SOME ASSEMBLY REQUIRED

SOME ASSEMBLY REQUIRED

FRESH *and* EASY NO-COOK RECIPES

❱ JULIA RUTLAND ❰

Adventure Publications

TABLE OF CONTENTS

Introduction 1

▶ APPETIZERS
Quick, Fresh Heirloom Salsa. 14
Chipotle-Lime Guacamole 15
Cranberry Salsa. 16
Roasted Red Pepper Hummus 17
Pineapple Salsa. 18
Lemon-Ricotta Lima Bean Dip 19
Muhammara
  (Roasted Red Bell Pepper Dip). 20
Smoky Salmon Dip 21
Watermelon-Feta-Cucumber Bites
  with Balsamic Glaze. 22
Marinated Peppers
  with Capers and Basil 23
Peach-and-Blue Cheese Crostini
  with Balsamic Glaze. 24
Beet-and-Goat Cheese Crostini 25
Smoked Salmon Bruschetta
  with Arugula Pesto. 26
Smoky Cheddar-Pecan Cheese Ball . . . 27
Cóctel de Camarones 28
Chilled Shrimp with Two Sauces. 29
Sun-dried Tomato-and-Pesto Torta. . . . 30
Goat Cheese-and-Pistachio Grapes . . . 32
Smoky Chipotle-Bacon
  Deviled Eggs 33
West Indies Crab Salad 34
Smoked Trout Dip. 35
Southern Pickled Shrimp. 36

▶ BEVERAGES
Hibiscus Tea Lemonade. 40
Watermelon Agua Fresca 41
Tropical Sangría 42
White Linen Cocktail 43
Tiki Blush. 44
Frozen Gin and Tonic 45

Mocha Punch. 46
Bushwhacker Shake 47
Limoncello Mojito. 48
Whiskey Amaretto Slushie. 49

▶ BREAKFAST
Creamy Kale-and-Cashew Smoothie . . 52
Brown Sugar-Cinnamon
  Overnight Oatmeal. 53
Open-Faced Avocado-Egg Salad
  Sandwich. 54
Smoked Salmon Breakfast Wrap 55
No-Bake Chocolate-Almond
  Breakfast Cookies. 56

▶ SANDWICHES AND WRAPS
Dilled Egg Salad 60
Pimiento Cheese 61
Elevated Cream Cheese-and-Olive
  Sandwiches 62
Ham Salad 63
Turkey with Rosemary-Orange
  Marmalade Sauce. 64
Bahn Mi Sandwiches. 65
Lemony Lobster Rolls 66
Chicken, Prosciutto, and Goat Cheese
  Sandwiches 67
Mediterranean Hummus Wrap
  with Vinaigrette. 68
Greek Chicken-and-Zucchini Wrap 69
No-Cook Chicken (Larb)
  Salad Wraps. 70
Veggie Summer Rolls
  with Hoisin Peanut Sauce 72
Spicy Lentil Lettuce Wraps 73
Chicken-and-Black Bean Tostadas 74

▶ SOUPS
Spicy Garden Veggie Soup 78
Chilled Cucumber Soup 79

Chilled Avocado Soup....................80
Golden Tomato-and-Peach Gazpacho..........................81
All-the-Red-Things Chilled Soup (Tomato-Watermelon-Berry Gazpacho)..........................82
Chilled Zucchini-and-Basil Soup.......84
White Gazpacho with Cucumber (Ajo Blanco Verde)...................85

❯ SALADS AND SIDES

Tomato Salad with Herbed Buttermilk Dressing............................88
Marinated Heirloom Tomatoes with Burrata.......................89
Tomato-and-Avocado Salad............90
Wedge Salad with Buttermilk-Blue Cheese Dressing............................91
Cantaloupe-and-Blueberry Salad with Honey, Lime, and Mint..........92
Creamy Cucumber-and-Sweet Onion Salad.................................93
Celery Salad with Dates, Walnuts, and Parmesan..........................94
Marinated Celery-and-Chickpea Salad with Lemon-Shallot Vinaigrette......95
Cauliflower Chickpea Salad Bowl with Curry-Tahini Dressing..........96
Hearts of Palm, Grapefruit, and Avocado Salad......................97
Couscous-Tabbouleh Salad...........98
Mediterranean White Bean Salad......99
Heirloom Tomato Panzanella with Brie and Basil................100
Moroccan Kale-and-Grain Salad with Cumin-Coriander Vinaigrette...102
Strawberry-Spinach Salad with Toasted Pecans and Honey-Poppy Seed Dressing...........................103
Chopped Salad with Avocado-Ranch Dressing...........................104

Simple Side Salad with Blended Ginger Dressing...........................105
Kale Salad with Orange-Sesame Dressing...........................106
Bibb Salad with Raspberries, Mango, Hazelnuts, Goat Cheese, and Raspberry Vinaigrette..........107
Beet, Orange, and Blue Cheese Salad with Tarragon Vinaigrette...........108
Simple Beet-and-Arugula Salad with Whipped Ricotta and Honey Vinaigrette.........................109
Carrot, Mango, and Jicama Slaw.......110
Tex-Mex Coleslaw with Creamy Lime-Chipotle Dressing.............111
Ramen Noodle Slaw..................112

❯ MAIN-DISH SALADS AND BOWLS

Lemony Herbed Chicken Salad........116
Quick Curried Chicken Salad..........117
Chicken Waldorf Salad................118
Southern Chicken, Tomato, and Black-eyed Pea Salad...........119
Easy Chicken Cobb Salad with Dijon Vinaigrette..............120
Mexican Chicken Cobb Salad with Chipotle Ranch Dressing......122
Chicken Caesar Salad with Chipotle Dressing.............123
Crispy Fried Chicken Salad with Honey-Mustard Dressing......124
Chicken-and-Napa Cabbage Salad with Sesame-Soy Vinaigrette.......125
Chicken, Orange, and Hazelnut Salad Bowl with Honey-Orange Dressing...........................126
Chicken-and-Grain Bowl with Creamy Green Goddess Dressing............127
Spicy Chicken-and-Mango Salad Bowl with Cilantro-Lime Vinaigrette......128

TABLE OF CONTENTS

Chicken Noodle Bowl
  with Peanut-Coconut Dressing..... 129
Chicken Salad Bowl
  with Five-Spice Vinaigrette 130
Chicken Burrito Bowl
  with Creamy Chipotle Dressing 131
Greek Chicken Rice Bowl
  with Tzatziki Dressing 132
Za'atar Chicken, Bulgur,
  and Lentil Salad Bowl 134
Salad Bowl with Curried Miso
  Dressing 135
Steak, Corn, and Tomato Salad
  with Smoky Cumin Vinaigrette...... 136
Beefsteak Salad with Blue Cheese-
  Balsamic Vinaigrette 137
Roast Beef Salad with Heirloom Tomatoes
  and Thai Dressing.................. 138
Watercress-and-Roast Beef Salad
  with Chimichurri Vinaigrette 139
Hearty Cuban Salad
  with Mojo Vinaigrette 140
Antipasto Salad with Marinated
  Artichokes, Beans, Slivered Meats,
  and Creamy Hummus Dressing......141
Tuna Niçoise Salad
  with Caper-Shallot Vinaigrette...... 142
Fall Greens with Smoked Trout, Pear,
  Cranberry, and Date Vinaigrette 143
Smoked Sockeye Caesar Salad
  with Lemony Dressing 144
Quinoa-and-Smoked Salmon Kale Bowl
  with Lemon-Tahini Dressing........ 145
Smoked Salmon-and-Beet Salad
  with Gribiche Dressing 146
California Roll Bowl 147
Shrimp-and-Glass Noodle Salad 148
Shrimp-and-Hoppin' John Salad...... 149
Crawfish Rémoulade.................. 150

▶ **DESSERTS**

No-Churn Mixed-Berry Ice Cream 154
Super Quick-and-Easy
  Peach Sherbet..................... 155
Chocolate-Hazelnut Ice Cream 156
Chocolate Brownie-Batter
  Hummus 157
Tiramisu.............................. 158
Strawberry-Brownie Trifle Cups....... 159
Raspberry-and-Lemon
  Icebox Cake 160
Berry-Cheesecake Cups 162
No-Bake Chocolate Cheesecake with
  Chocolate Cookie Crust 163
Gingersnap-and-Berries Tart 164
Lemon Icebox Pie.................... 165
No-Bake Banana Cream Pie
  with Chocolate Layer.............. 166
Frozen Peanut Butter Pie............ 167
Possum Pie.......................... 168
Chocolate-Covered
  Pecan Pie Balls 170
No-Bake Chocolate-Topped
  Peanut Butter-Oat Cups............171
Raw Pecan-and-Date Brownies 172

Equivalents................... 174
Index 180
About the Author................ 192

ACKNOWLEDGMENTS

I am deeply grateful to everyone who supported me in the creation of this cookbook. To my family—Dit, Corinne, Bishop, and Nick—your encouragement and willingness to sample my culinary experiments (and run to the market) helped beyond words. A heartfelt thank-you to the incredible team at AdventureKEEN—Molly, Brett, Emily, Hilary, and Megan—for your expert guidance, unwavering dedication, and hard work in bringing this project to life.

I'm especially grateful to the friends who generously shared their time and taste buds to test recipes—your honest feedback and enthusiasm made the process both successful and truly fun. Special thanks to Cynthia, Jeff, Ingrid, Joe, Vicki, John, Kristin, Ikumi, Jey, and Leslie. Thank you, Beth, for your guidance and inspiration—the handwoven napkins and towels pictured in these pages were created in your class. To the members of the Fiber Guild of the Blue Ridge and the Loudoun County Master Gardeners—thank you for happily sampling many of the dishes at the potlucks and other get-togethers.

And a special nod of appreciation goes to Mary Beth Shaddix, who offered steady encouragement against a gorgeous Lake Martin backdrop in Alabama, back when this idea was just a seed.

INTRODUCTION

I'm so excited to finally share *Some Assembly Required*, a collection of no-cook recipes that I've been wanting to create for years. This book celebrates the kind of food prep I love most during the heat of summer—simple, satisfying dishes that don't require turning on the stove or oven. When the temperatures rise, the last thing I want to do is heat up the house. Even grilling, as tasty as it is, still means standing over a hot flame. No-cook meals are my go-to during the warmest months, and they also happen to be perfect for outdoor adventures like camping—one of my favorite ways to vacation.

Inside this book you'll find a little bit of everything: appetizers and beverages for entertaining or relaxing on the porch; refreshing chilled soups, sandwiches, and sides; protein-packed salads that make a full meal; and even a few cool-and-creative desserts. Each recipe is designed to be simple and flexible, making it easy to put together a great dish without breaking a sweat.

No-cook meals also happen to be the best way I know to stretch leftovers and save time. I don't just repurpose extra ingredients—I plan for them. If I'm grilling chicken, I make a few extra pieces to use later in a salad or wrap. I freeze leftover rice and quinoa in small portions to have at the ready for quick bowls or side dishes. Rotisserie chicken, steamed shrimp from the seafood counter, canned beans, and precooked grains are all building blocks I rely on. These kinds of shortcuts make everyday meals easier without sacrificing flavor or nutrition.

Whether you're trying to stay cool, save time, or avoid a pile of dirty dishes, I hope this book brings fresh inspiration to your table.

When the weather heats up or time is short, no-cook meals are a refreshing, practical way to make meals simple and easy. The recipes in this book rely on fresh, ready-to-eat ingredients that require no stove, oven, or grill—just a bit of chopping, layering, or blending. From vibrant dips and hearty salads to chilled soups, sandwiches, and wraps, no-cook recipes prove that terrific flavor doesn't have to come from heat.

No-cook recipes are ideal for busy days, warm weather, or anytime you want to keep things simple. These easy meals are:

Time-saving: No-cook recipes come together quickly, making them perfect for busy weeknights, last-minute meals, or when you're too tired to cook. With no need to preheat an oven or wait for water to boil, you can go from ingredients to a plated meal in minutes.

Heat-free: On hot days, turning on the stove or oven can make your kitchen feel unbearable. No-cook recipes keep things cool and comfortable, helping you avoid adding extra heat to your home while still enjoying a fresh, satisfying meal.

Low on cleanup: Since there's no cooking involved, you'll typically only need a cutting board, knife, mixing bowl, and maybe a blender. Fewer dishes mean less time spent washing up and more time enjoying your meal or relaxing afterward.

High on freshness: No-cook meals often highlight raw or minimally processed ingredients like fruits, vegetables, herbs, and simple proteins. This makes them naturally lighter, more refreshing, and a great way to increase your intake of seasonal produce.

Versatile: These meals can be easily adjusted based on what you have in your fridge or pantry. Swap in different vegetables, grains, or proteins depending on your preferences or dietary needs—there's no strict formula.

Travel-friendly: No-cook dishes are great for packing up and taking to picnics, potlucks, or lunch at work. Because there's nothing hot to spill or keep warm, they transport well and can be enjoyed cold or at room temperature.

Kid- and beginner-friendly: Without hot surfaces or complicated techniques, these meals are safer and easier for children and novice cooks to help with or prepare on their own. No-cook meals are a great way to build kitchen confidence and get the whole family involved.

Energy-efficient: Not using gas or electricity to cook your food means these recipes are kinder to your utility bill—and the environment. They're an easy way to cut down on energy use without sacrificing any flavor or variety.

MEAL PREP TIPS FOR NO-COOK MEALS

Meal prep is a powerful way to make no-cook meals even more convenient and stress-free. By washing and chopping produce, preparing sauces, and portioning out ingredients ahead of time, you can reduce the daily effort needed for meal assembly. Having components like prepped vegetables, cooked grains, and ready-to-use proteins on hand means you can mix and match ingredients quickly, avoid food waste, and maintain variety throughout the week—all without ever turning on the stove.

Stock the pantry with ready-to-use items: Keep staples like canned beans, olives, tuna, nut butters, jarred roasted peppers, dried fruits, and grains like couscous or precooked rice available for easy assembly.

Wash and prep produce in advance: Rinse leafy greens, chop vegetables, and wash berries or herbs ahead of time. Store them in airtight containers or zip-top plastic bags so they're ready to grab and use.

Use precooked proteins or deli options: Rotisserie chicken, smoked salmon, hard-boiled eggs, and sliced deli meats are convenient sources of protein that don't require cooking. Tofu, canned lentils, or marinated tempeh are great plant-based options.

Make versatile sauces and dressings: Blend up vinaigrettes, tahini sauces, yogurt dips, or pestos that can be used across multiple meals. Store them in glass jars and use throughout the week to add flavor to wraps, salads, or bowls.

Prep grain or pasta bases ahead: While technically cooked, grains like quinoa, rice, or pasta can be prepared in bulk ahead of time and used chilled. (See instructions on page 8.) Keep them refrigerated or frozen and ready to toss with veggies, beans, or dressings.

Portion out snacks or meal components: Divide hummus, cut fruit, trail mix, or salad toppers like nuts and seeds into single servings for easy grab-and-go options or into compartmentalized containers like bento boxes for lunchtime.

Organize a no-cook meal board or list: Keep a list of favorite combinations or recipes you can make with what you have on hand. This saves time when deciding what to eat and helps reduce food waste.

Use storage containers that work for you: Clear containers make it easy to see what's prepped and ready to eat. Label with dates so ingredients stay fresh and organized.

ESSENTIAL KITCHEN EQUIPMENT FOR NO-COOK MEALS

No-cook meals may be simple to assemble, but having the right kitchen tools at the ready can make the process even more enjoyable. From prepping fresh produce to blending sauces or storing leftovers, a few key pieces of equipment can streamline your workflow and expand what you're able to create without turning on the stove. These tools are especially useful for building up flavor and texture while keeping your kitchen cool.

Chef's Knife and Paring Knife: A sharp chef's knife is your most important tool for slicing vegetables, fruits, and proteins efficiently and safely. A smaller paring knife is also helpful for more detailed work like peeling, segmenting citrus, or trimming herbs and fruit.

Cutting Board: A sturdy cutting board provides a clean, stable surface for chopping and prepping ingredients. It's helpful to have more than one—one for produce and another for cheese or meats—to keep flavors and textures clean.

Blender: Ideal for smoothies, dressings, dips, and chilled soups like gazpacho or white bean puree, a high-powered blender can also handle frozen fruits and fibrous veggies for ultrasmooth results.

Immersion Blender: Also known as a stick blender, this tool is a time-saver because it lets you blend soups, sauces, and smoothies directly in the pot or container—there's no need to transfer batches to a traditional blender and clean extra dishes. It's fast, efficient, and perfect for quick blending jobs with minimal mess.

Food Processor: Great for chopping, shredding, and pureeing with minimal effort, use it to make hummus, dips, or to pulse ingredients for energy bites or piecrusts.

Salad Spinner: Crisp greens are a staple in many no-cook meals, and a salad spinner helps wash and thoroughly dry lettuce, herbs, and other leafy produce. Dry leaves hold salad dressings better and stay fresher longer in the fridge.

Mandolin Slicer: This tool provides quick, uniform slices of vegetables and fruits—perfect for raw salads, slaws, or garnishes. Use with caution and a hand guard for safety, especially when slicing thinly.

Vegetable Peeler: Essential for peeling or shaving vegetables like carrots, zucchini, or cucumbers into ribbons, some peelers can also julienne to create noodle-like textures in raw salads.

Mixing Bowls: These are useful for tossing salads, assembling wraps, or combining dips and spreads. Look for nesting bowls that save space and are easy to clean.

Citrus Juicer or Reamer: These add efficiency and minimize mess when squeezing fresh lemon, lime, or orange juice for dressings, marinades, or beverages. My favorite is a manual handheld press that resembles tongs with a bowl at the end. It uses leverage to squeeze every last drop of juice!

Microplane: Sometimes called a zester, these ultrasharp gadgets grate the zest from citrus quickly without digging into the bitter white pith.

Storage Containers: Handy for storing prepped ingredients, leftover dips, or layered salads, clear containers help you stay organized and reduce waste by making it easy to see what's ready to eat. I prefer glass options because they don't absorb odors or stains, keeping food fresh without affecting flavor.

Canning Jars: These are great for making salad dressings because they seal tightly, allow for easy shaking to mix ingredients, and double as convenient storage containers.

Hot Water Dispenser (Built-In or Electric): While not traditionally part of a no-cook setup, a hot water dispenser brings next-level convenience. It provides near-boiling water on demand—great for making tea, pour-over coffee, instant ramen, cellophane noodles, or couscous. Though built-in models can be expensive to install, they're a worthwhile upgrade if you regularly drink hot beverages or prepare quick-cook items. I'm so enamored with this device, I've learned to install one myself when updating or moving to a new house.

Vacuum Sealer: As another unexpected tool for no-cook meals, a vacuum sealer is useful because it extends the freshness of precooked ingredients and leftovers, making it easy to prep in advance. Cooked foods can be portioned, sealed, and frozen, then quickly thawed and assembled without any extra cooking.

chef's knife

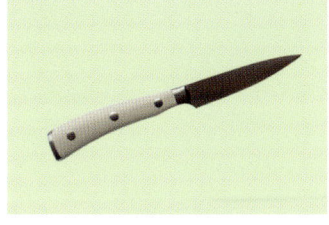
paring knife

cutting board

blender

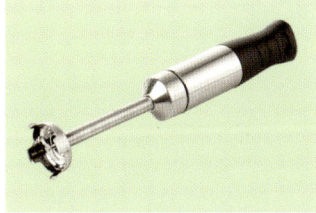
immersion blender

food processor

salad spinner

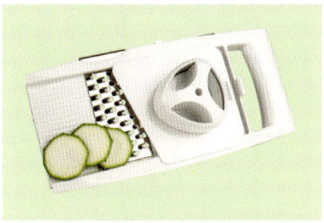
mandolin slicer

vegetable peeler

mixing bowls

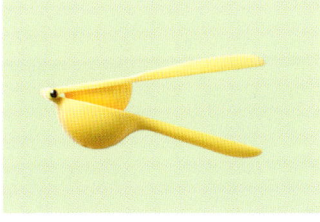
citrus juicer or reamer

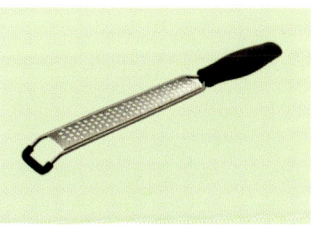
microplane

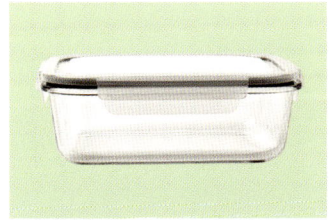
Storage containers

canning jars

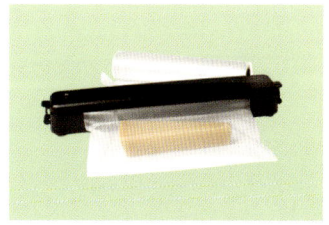
vacuum sealer

COOKED PROTEIN OPTIONS

When you're assembling no-cook meals, having a variety of precooked protein options on hand can make all the difference. These ready-to-eat choices save time and effort while still providing substance and nourishment. Whether you prefer animal-based proteins, plant-based alternatives, or a mix of both, these convenient options can be used straight from the fridge or pantry with no additional prep required.

- **Rotisserie Chicken:** This versatile-and-flavorful staple can be shredded or chopped for wraps, salads, grain bowls, or sandwiches.

- **Steamed Shrimp and Other Cooked Seafood:** If your grocery store has a seafood counter that offers cooked, ready-to-eat shrimp, crab, mussels, or salmon fillets, these can be used in salads, lettuce cups, or seafood rolls. You can also find cooked seafood like shrimp, crawfish, and crab in the freezer section.

- **Deli Meats:** Sliced turkey, ham, roast beef, pastrami, and salami are easy to roll into wraps, layer on sandwiches, or chop and toss into salads.

- **Ready-to-Eat Cooked Chicken Strips/Tenders:** Found in the deli area (near the bacon and sliced meats), these can be tossed into salads or grain bowls. Many come presliced and grilled or lightly breaded. You'll find major brands like Tyson, Bell & Evans, Purdue, Springer, Trader Joe's, and Applegate, as well as generic brands. The same brands often sell precooked chicken strips in the freezer section. They thaw quickly, but for added food safety, reheat the frozen-and-thawed versions to an internal temperature of 165°F before using in recipes.

- **Hard-Boiled Eggs:** Sold peeled, these are a wonderfully convenient protein source for salads, sandwiches, or egg salad. Find these in packages near the cartons of eggs at the grocery store.

- **Tofu (Plain or Marinated):** Firm tofu can be cubed and eaten straight from the package or marinated for extra flavor.

- **Smoked Tofu:** Already seasoned and firmer in texture, smoked tofu has a savory, hearty flavor that's great in wraps or salads.

- **Tempeh:** This fermented soy product is typically precooked and can be sliced thin and added to sandwiches, bowls, or cold noodle dishes.

- **Canned Beans and Lentils:** Black beans, chickpeas, white beans, or lentils can be rinsed and added directly to salads, dips, or wraps.

- **Canned Tuna, Salmon, or Chicken:** Great pantry staples that require no prep, these can be combined with mayonnaise, mustard, or herbs for a quick protein-packed spread or salad.

- **Smoked Salmon, Lox, and Other Seafood:** Use these to add a savory, briny bite to bagels, salads, or wraps. Smoked trout is less readily available—try large or higher end stores; it's sometimes available at Trader Joe's. Another precooked seafood product you'll find nearby is surimi or faux "crab." It's extremely mild and often quite affordable.

- **Plant-Based Deli Slices or Meat Alternatives:** Many brands offer cooked vegan "turkey," "ham," or "chicken" slices that are ready to eat and can be used just like traditional deli meats.

- **Cheese:** While not high in protein per ounce, cheeses like mozzarella, cheddar, or feta add a flavorful boost and can round out a vegetarian no-cook meal.

PRECOOKED PANTRY ITEMS

For no-cook meals to come together quickly, a well-stocked pantry is key. Keeping shelf-stable, precooked ingredients stocked means you can easily assemble satisfying meals. Whether you're building a salad, wrap, grain bowl, or snack plate, these convenient staples offer flavor, nutrition, and flexibility with zero cooking required.

- **Canned Beans:** Black beans, chickpeas, kidney beans, white beans, and lentils can be drained and rinsed for immediate use.
- **Canned Lentils:** A quick plant-based protein that's already tender, lentils are great in grain bowls, Mediterranean salads, or mashed into spreads.
- **Precooked Grains (pouches, vacuum-sealed, or jarred):** These packets of white or brown rice, quinoa, farro, barley, or couscous are shelf-stable and microwaveable but also fine to eat cold in salads or bowls. Look for flavored or international varieties with ample seasoning.
- **Canned Tuna, Salmon, or Chicken:** These are fully cooked and ready to mix into salads and spreads. Or you can serve them on crackers or toast.
- **Shelf-Stable Tofu (Silken or Firm):** Silken tofu is great for creamy dips or smoothies, while firm varieties can be cubed for salads or grain bowls.
- **Marinated Vegetables and Legumes (Jarred or Canned):** Items like marinated artichoke hearts, roasted red peppers, white bean salads, and pickled beets add flavor and bulk without extra cooking.
- **Nut Butters (Peanut, Almond, Cashew, etc.):** High in protein and fat, these are perfect for spreading on bread, drizzling over fruit, or stirring into sauces or dips. Some brands add chocolate for a yummy dessert-friendly option.
- **Shelf-Stable Hummus or Bean Dips:** Some brands sell single-serve or vacuum-packed hummus, baba ghanoush, or lentil spreads that don't require refrigeration until after they're opened.

- **Instant Couscous or Bulgur Wheat:** These grains cook quickly with just hot water, or you can soak them in room-temperature water for longer to hydrate without heat.

HOME-COOKED RICE AND GRAINS

Some prepackaged cooked grains and rice can be dry and surprisingly expensive. I prefer to plan ahead and cook my own. When cooking rice for any meal, I make enough for leftovers, then store it for easy use later. After cooking according to package directions, spread grains or rice in a shallow layer so that it cools quickly. Portion it into 1- to 2-cup servings, then transfer to an airtight container. If you are working with leftovers, do not allow the grains or rice to remain on the counter for more than 2 hours (and ideally much less) because bacteria thrive in the "danger zone" between 40°F and 140°F.

Cooked rice and grains may be refrigerated safely for about 3 days—though I personally prefer to serve or discard it after a day (my chickens love it!) to maintain peak flavor and texture. For longer storage, freeze it for 2 to 3 months. Vacuum sealing reduces freezer burn. If you don't have a vacuum sealer, place the cooled, cooked rice in a zip-top plastic storage bag and press to remove as much air as possible before freezing. Thaw in the refrigerator. **Bonus:** Cooked and cooled rice encourages the formation of resistant starch, which lowers the glycemic spike one gets after eating it.

FOOD SAFETY

When serving cold foods like salads at potlucks and buffets, food safety is just as important as flavor. To prevent the growth of harmful bacteria, it's essential to keep perishable dishes at the proper temperature. Cold foods should be kept at 40°F or below, whether by using ice-filled trays, insulated coolers, or frequent replenishing from a refrigerated source.

Following a few simple precautions can help to ensure that your dishes stay safe to eat and everyone goes home with good memories—not a foodborne illness.

- Keep cold foods at 40°F or below by using ice packs or coolers, or by nesting serving bowls in trays of ice.

- Transport cold dishes in insulated containers to maintain a safe temperature during travel.

- Avoid leaving cold foods out without temperature control (i.e., on ice) for more than 2 hours (or 1 hour if the outdoor temperature is above 90°F).

- Serve smaller portions and keep reserved amounts chilled, refilling as needed.

- Use a thermometer to check that foods stay at or below 40°F during the party.

- Label coolers clearly if you're using more than one, so guests don't frequently open those holding cold items when they're searching for something else.

FRESHNESS GUIDELINES

Keeping ingredients fresh is key to successful no-cook meals. Knowing how long different items last in the fridge or freezer can help you plan better, avoid waste, and ensure your meals are safe and flavorful.

Before storing, cool cooked food quickly by spreading it into a thin layer on a clean baking sheet. That will release heat fast and prevent bacterial growth. Once cooked (within 1 to 2 hours), transfer to containers, label with date and contents listed, and refrigerator or freeze.

FRESHNESS GUIDELINES

INGREDIENT	REFRIGERATOR	FREEZER
Vegetables and Fruits		
Leafy Greens	3 to 5 days (store in a salad spinner or bag)	Not recommended (texture suffers)
Herbs	3 to 5 days (in a jar with water, covered loosely)	Up to 2 months (chop and freeze in oil or water)
Cucumbers	4 to 6 days	Not recommended (becomes mushy)
Bell Peppers	4 to 6 days	Up to 6 months (slice and freeze)
Carrots	5 to 7 days	Up to 6 months (peel and slice before freezing)
Berries	2 to 4 days (unwashed before use)	Up to 6 months (wash, dry, and freeze)
Tomatoes	3 to 5 days once ripe	Not recommended unless used for sauce
Avocados	2 to 3 days once ripe	Up to 6 months (freeze mashed with lemon juice)
Meats		
Rotisserie or Cooked Chicken	3 to 4 days	3 to 6 months
Steamed Shrimp	2 to 3 days	Up to 2 months
Deli Meats	3 to 5 days after opening	Up to 2 months (freeze in portions)
Hard-Boiled Eggs	1 week (peeled or unpeeled)	Not recommended
Egg, Tuna, Chicken, or Ham Salad	3 to 5 days	Not recommended
Grains		
Barley	3 to 5 days	Up to 3 months (best if frozen with broth)
Couscous	3 to 5 days	Up to 3 months
Farro	3 to 5 days	Up to 3 months
Quinoa	5 to 7 days	Up to 3 months
White or Brown Rice	3 days	Up to 6 months (cool before freezing)
Wild Rice	5 to 6 days	Up to 6 months

TIPS FOR STORING PRODUCE

- **Use your crisper drawers wisely:** Most refrigerators have two crisper drawers with adjustable humidity. Store fruits in the low-humidity drawer and vegetables in the high-humidity drawer to slow moisture loss and spoilage.

- **Separate ethylene-producing fruits:** Apples, bananas, avocados, peaches, pears, and tomatoes emit ethylene gas, which can speed up ripening (and spoilage) of nearby produce. Keep them away from ethylene-sensitive items like leafy greens, berries, carrots, and broccoli.

- **Don't wash produce until ready to use:** Moisture encourages mold and decay. For the best shelf life, wait to wash delicate items like berries or herbs until just before eating them.

- **Store herbs like flowers:** Treat tender herbs (like parsley, cilantro, and basil) like cut flowers: Trim the ends, place them in a jar of water, and loosely cover with a plastic bag. Refrigerate most herbs—but keep basil at room temperature to prevent browning, as basil is sensitive to low temperatures.

- **Keep produce in breathable bags or containers:** Use perforated bags or containers designed for produce to allow air circulation while retaining the right amount of moisture.

- **Keep mushrooms in paper bags:** Paper bags help absorb excess moisture and keep mushrooms from becoming slimy. Avoid plastic, which traps moisture and accelerates spoilage.

- **Use root vegetables wisely:** Carrots, beets, and radishes store well in the crisper drawer. Remove any leafy tops first—they draw moisture from the roots—and store them separately or discard.

- **Store onions and garlic in a cool, dry place:** Keep them in a well-ventilated basket or mesh bag, away from potatoes (which can cause sprouting). Do not refrigerate them unless they've been cut.

STORING MEAT AND DAIRY
Meat (Cooked and Uncooked)

Store on the lowest refrigerator shelf: Keep raw meats in leak-proof containers on the bottom shelf to prevent juices from dripping onto other foods and causing cross-contamination.

Follow safe storage times:

Raw Poultry and Ground Meat: 1 to 2 days in the fridge

Raw Beef, Pork, Lamb: 3 to 5 days

Cooked Meats: 3 to 4 days

Deli Meats: 3 to 5 days after opening

Freeze if not using soon: Freeze meats in airtight packaging or zip-top plastic freezer bags to prevent freezer burn. Label with the type and date for easy reference. Most cooked and raw meats keep well in the freezer for 3 to 6 months.

Thaw safely: Thaw in the refrigerator, not on the counter. For quicker thawing, use the microwave or a sealed bag in cold water, but cook immediately afterward.

Dairy Products

Store in the coldest part of the fridge: The back of a middle shelf (not the door) maintains the most consistent temperature. Avoid storing milk or yogurt in the door where temps fluctuate.

Keep containers tightly sealed: Reseal or cover cheese, yogurt, sour cream, and milk after each use to prevent odor absorption and slow down spoilage.

Know typical shelf life:

- Milk: 5–7 days after opening
- Yogurt: 1–2 weeks after opening
- Cheese (hard): 3–4 weeks after opening
- Cheese (soft): 1–2 weeks
- Butter: 1–3 months refrigerated; up to 6 months frozen

Freeze selectively: Hard cheeses and butter freeze well; milk and soft cheeses can freeze, but their texture may change. Shred cheese before freezing for easier use later.

Check for spoilage: Look for sour smells, mold (except on naturally moldy cheeses like blue cheese), or separation in dairy products. When in doubt, throw it out!

STORAGE CONTAINERS

Glass Containers

- Best for hot foods or reheating, glass containers are the gold standard for all food storage. Never heat or reheat food in plastic containers, as some can leach chemicals when exposed to high temperatures.

- Glass is nonporous, doesn't absorb odors, and resists staining from foods like tomato sauce or those containing spices like curry or turmeric.

- Choose containers with airtight lids for longer freshness and less risk of spills.

Plastic Containers

- These are best for cold storage, packed lunches, or lightweight transport.

- Lightweight and shatter-resistant, plastic containers are convenient but should be used only for cold or room-temperature foods. Look for BPA-free labels and avoid reheating in plastic to minimize chemical exposure.

- Replace plastic containers when they become stained, warped, or scratched.

Reusable Silicone or Zip-Top Plastic Bags

- These are best for storing chopped produce, marinated proteins, nuts, and other snacks.

- Reusable silicone bags are flexible, eco-friendly alternatives to plastic and are freezer- and dishwasher-safe. Disposable plastic bags are convenient but should be used sparingly and never reused for raw meats.

- Press out as much air as possible before sealing for best storage results.

APPETIZERS

36

14 Quick, Fresh Heirloom Salsa
15 Chipotle-Lime Guacamole
16 Cranberry Salsa
17 Roasted Red Pepper Hummus
18 Pineapple Salsa
19 Lemon-Ricotta Lima Bean Dip
20 Muhammara (Roasted Red Bell Pepper Dip)
21 Smoky Salmon Dip
22 Watermelon-Feta-Cucumber Bites with Balsamic Glaze
23 Marinated Peppers with Capers and Basil
24 Peach-and-Blue Cheese Crostini with Balsamic Glaze
25 Beet-and-Goat Cheese Crostini
26 Smoked Salmon Bruschetta with Arugula Pesto
27 Smoky Cheddar-Pecan Cheese Ball
28 Cóctel de Camarones
29 Chilled Shrimp with Two Sauces
30 Sun-dried Tomato-and-Pesto Torta
32 Goat Cheese-and-Pistachio Grapes
33 Smoky Chipotle-Bacon Deviled Eggs
34 West Indies Crab Salad
35 Smoked Trout Dip
36 Southern Pickled Shrimp

33

24

27

QUICK, FRESH HEIRLOOM SALSA

MAKES 4 CUPS

½ red onion, coarsely chopped

1 jalapeño pepper, seeded and coarsely chopped

3 garlic cloves, coarsely chopped

½ cup lightly packed fresh cilantro leaves

1 teaspoon grated lime zest

3 tablespoons fresh lime juice

1½ teaspoons fine sea salt

½ teaspoon ground cumin

4 large heirloom or beefsteak tomatoes, coarsely chopped

Garnish: fresh cilantro sprigs

Tortilla chips

This zesty tomato salsa is bursting with flavor and can be easily customized to your preference. Keep it chunky for a classic pico de gallo texture or blend it until smooth for a restaurant-style salsa. Either way, it's perfect for dipping with tortilla chips, spooning over tacos, or serving alongside grilled meats.

Combine onion, jalapeño, garlic, cilantro, lime zest and juice, salt, and cumin in a food processor. Pulse until evenly chopped. Add tomatoes; pulse several times until evenly chopped and well blended. Garnish, if desired, and serve with tortilla chips.

CHIPOTLE-LIME GUACAMOLE

MAKES 2½ CUPS

Smoky, bright, and irresistibly creamy, this dip is a bold twist on the classic with its flavorful balance of spice and tang. Adjust the chipotle peppers to suit your crowd.

4 ripe avocados, halved
2 teaspoons grated lime zest
3 tablespoons fresh lime juice
1 teaspoon fine sea salt
¾ teaspoon ground cumin
2 tablespoons chopped red onion
1 tablespoon minced chipotle peppers in adobo sauce
Garnishes: lime slices, red onion slices
Tortilla chips

1. Scoop out avocado halves from skins and place into a bowl. Add lime zest and juice, salt, and cumin. Mash avocado with a fork until well blended.
2. Add onion and chipotle peppers, stirring until well blended. Cover guacamole with plastic wrap and chill until ready to serve. Garnish, if desired, and serve with tortilla chips.

CRANBERRY SALSA

MAKES 2 CUPS

1 seedless orange

1 (12-ounce) bag fresh or frozen cranberries, thawed

⅓ cup granulated sugar

¼ cup coarsely chopped sweet onion

1 jalapeño, coarsely chopped

½ teaspoon fine sea salt

⅓ cup fresh cilantro leaves

Garnishes: fresh cilantro sprigs, orange slices

Sweet potato chips

Fresh cranberries have a limited season, but they freeze well for months, so I tend to keep a bag on hand for those hot summer days when the tart berry is most welcome and refreshing.

Grate orange peel to yield 2 teaspoons orange zest. Segment orange. Add zest and orange segments, cranberries, sugar, onion, jalapeño, and salt to the bowl of a food processor; pulse until evenly chopped. Add cilantro and pulse until combined. Garnish, if desired, and serve with sweet potato chips.

ROASTED RED PEPPER HUMMUS

This slightly smoky hummus is just the right consistency for dipping with pita chips, spreading on sandwiches, or serving alongside fresh vegetables.

MAKES 1¾ CUPS

- 1 (15-ounce) can chickpeas, rinsed and drained
- 1 jarred roasted red bell pepper, drained and cut into pieces
- ½ teaspoon grated lemon zest
- 3 tablespoons fresh lemon juice
- ⅓ cup tahini
- 1 garlic clove, chopped
- 2 tablespoons extra-virgin olive oil
- 1 teaspoon ground cumin
- 1 teaspoon fine sea salt
- ¼ teaspoon smoked paprika or ground cayenne pepper
- Garnishes: lemon slices, cracked black pepper
- Soft pita triangles

Combine chickpeas, bell pepper, lemon zest and juice, tahini, garlic, oil, cumin, salt, and paprika in a food processor. Process until smooth and creamy. Garnish, if desired, and serve with soft pita triangles.

PINEAPPLE SALSA

MAKES ABOUT 6½ CUPS

- 1 small pineapple, peeled, cored, and coarsely chopped
- 1 small red bell pepper, coarsely chopped
- 1 jalapeño, seeded and minced
- ¼ cup minced red onion
- 1 teaspoon light brown sugar (optional)
- 1 teaspoon chili powder
- 1 teaspoon grated lime zest
- 2 tablespoons fresh lime juice
- 1 teaspoon fine sea salt
- ⅓ cup chopped fresh cilantro
- Garnish: fresh cilantro sprigs
- Tortilla chips

Try this refreshing tropical salsa with tortilla chips, grilled fish, or tacos. Since pineapples vary in sweetness, a touch of brown sugar can help balance the flavors if your fruit is on the tart side—but if it's already super sweet, you can leave it out.

Combine pineapple; bell pepper; jalapeño; onion; brown sugar, if desired; chili powder; lime zest and juice; and salt in a large bowl. Stir until well blended. Stir in cilantro. Cover and chill until ready to serve. Garnish, if desired, and serve with tortilla chips.

LEMON-RICOTTA LIMA BEAN DIP

MAKES 2½ CUPS

1 (12-ounce) bag frozen baby lima beans, thawed
1 garlic clove, coarsely chopped
2 teaspoons grated lemon zest
¼ cup fresh lemon juice
½ cup ricotta cheese
2 tablespoons extra-virgin olive oil
1 teaspoon fine sea salt
Garnishes: chopped red bell pepper, coarsely ground black pepper
Fresh vegetable sticks

This light alternative to hummus features mild, buttery lima beans blended with ricotta, lemon zest, and olive oil. The ricotta adds richness without heaviness, while the lemon zest brightens the flavor. Unlike traditional hummus, this dip skips the tahini, making it smooth and delicate with a slightly sweet nuttiness from the beans.

Combine beans, garlic, lemon zest and juice, ricotta, oil, and salt in a food processor; puree until smooth. Garnish, if desired, and serve with fresh vegetable sticks.

MUHAMMARA (ROASTED RED BELL PEPPER DIP)

MAKES 2½ CUPS

Traditionally from Syria, this rich, savory spread is slightly sweet with a touch of tang, making it a flavorful alternative to hummus or baba ghanoush. It's perfect when served as a dip for flatbread like naan, as a spread on sandwiches, or as a bold addition to mezze platters.

3 jarred roasted red bell peppers
1 garlic clove, coarsely chopped
¾ cup toasted walnut halves
½ cup fresh or panko breadcrumbs
3 tablespoons extra-virgin olive oil
2 tablespoons tomato paste
2 tablespoons pomegranate molasses
¾ teaspoon ground cumin
¾ teaspoon fine sea salt
¼ to ½ teaspoon ground cayenne pepper or Aleppo pepper
Garnish: chopped walnuts
Flatbread

Combine bell peppers, garlic, walnuts, breadcrumbs, oil, tomato paste, molasses, cumin, salt, and cayenne in a food processor. Process until mixture is finely blended. Garnish, if desired, and serve with flatbread.

SMOKY SALMON DIP

MAKES 1½ CUPS

4 ounces cream cheese, softened
½ cup sour cream
¼ teaspoon lemon zest
2 teaspoons fresh lemon juice
4 ounces hot smoked sockeye salmon, broken into pieces
1 tablespoon chopped fresh or 1 teaspoon dried dill
1 tablespoon capers
2 teaspoons finely chopped red onion
Garnish: fresh dill sprigs
Bagel chips

This creamy smoked salmon dip is an elegant, flavorful appetizer that comes together in minutes. It has a rich, slightly smoky taste that pairs beautifully with cream cheese and fresh herbs. For extra depth, try using cracked black pepper smoked salmon; for a spicier kick, opt for Cajun-seasoned smoked salmon. Serve it with crisp flatbread crackers or crunchy bagel chips for an irresistible snack.

Combine cream cheese, sour cream, and lemon zest and juice in a food processor. Pulse until well blended. Add salmon and dill. Pulse until evenly chopped. Add capers and onion; pulse only until blended. Garnish, if desired. Serve with bagel chips.

WATERMELON-FETA-CUCUMBER BITES WITH BALSAMIC GLAZE

MAKES 10 SERVINGS

These refreshing, no-cook appetizer bites offer a delicious balance of sweet, salty, and tangy flavors. Serve these on a platter with cocktail picks for a beautiful and fuss-free starter.

½ seedless watermelon, peeled and cut into 1-inch cubes

2 seedless cucumbers, peeled and cut into 1-inch cubes

8 ounces feta cheese, cut into 1-inch cubes

1 tablespoon lime juice

1 tablespoon honey

2 teaspoons slivered fresh mint

Balsamic Glaze (recipe at right) or store-bought version

Garnish: fresh mint sprigs

1. Arrange cubes of watermelon, cucumber, and feta on a plate or platter. If making ahead, cover and refrigerate at this point.

2. Before serving, stir together lime juice, honey, and fresh mint. Drizzle over cubes. Drizzle lightly with Balsamic Glaze. Garnish, if desired, and serve immediately.

Balsamic Glaze: Gently simmer **1 cup balsamic vinegar** and **1 tablespoon brown sugar or honey,** if desired, in a small saucepan over low heat for about 10 minutes until mixture is reduced by half and coats the back of a spoon.

MARINATED PEPPERS WITH CAPERS AND BASIL

MAKES 4 TO 6 SERVINGS

2 tablespoons extra-virgin olive oil
1 tablespoon red wine vinegar
1 tablespoon capers, rinsed and drained
1 small garlic clove, minced
¼ teaspoon fine sea salt
¼ teaspoon coarsely ground black pepper
⅛ to ¼ teaspoon crushed red pepper flakes
1 (12- to 16-ounce) jar roasted red bell peppers, drained and patted dry
¼ cup fresh basil leaves, torn
Garnish: fresh basil leaves

Sweet, smoky roasted red bell peppers are a pantry staple that add vibrant color and deep flavor to any dish. Using jarred roasted peppers makes this recipe incredibly quick and easy, eliminating the need for roasting and peeling fresh ones. Serve these marinated peppers as part of an antipasto platter, layered on sandwiches, or as a topping for grilled meats or crusty bread.

1. Whisk together oil, red wine vinegar, capers, garlic, salt, black pepper, and red pepper flakes in a bowl. Slice roasted red bell peppers into strips and add to olive oil mixture, tossing to coat. Cover and let stand for 30 minutes (or refrigerate overnight until ready to serve).

2. Toss basil into pepper mixture. Arrange peppers on a platter and drizzle with marinade. Garnish, if desired.

PEACH-AND-BLUE CHEESE CROSTINI WITH BALSAMIC GLAZE

MAKES 2½ DOZEN

1 cup ricotta cheese

½ cup crumbled blue cheese or gorgonzola

30 crostini or toasted French bread slices

½ cup arugula leaves

3 ripe peaches, peeled, pitted, and thinly sliced

Balsamic Glaze (page 22) or store-bought version

¼ cup finely chopped toasted walnuts

This effortless bruschetta combines a perfect balance of flavors. Simply assemble and serve—each bite delivers a delightful mix of creamy, tangy, and sweet. Look for prepared crostini in the deli section of grocery stores—they are usually fresher than bagged items.

1. Combine ricotta and blue cheese in a small food processor; process until smooth.

2. Spread about 2 teaspoons cheese mixture evenly onto each crostini. Top with a few arugula leaves and 1 to 2 peach slices. Drizzle with Balsamic Glaze and sprinkle with walnuts.

BEET-AND-GOAT CHEESE CROSTINI

MAKES 2 DOZEN

This gem-colored appetizer comes together effortlessly with the help of store-bought crostini and packaged refrigerated beets—there's no roasting or peeling required! Ideal for entertaining or a quick snack, these crostini offer a delicious balance of flavors and textures with minimal prep.

- 3 tablespoons extra-virgin olive oil
- ¼ cup white balsamic or white wine vinegar
- 1 tablespoon honey
- ½ teaspoon fine sea salt
- ¼ teaspoon coarsely ground black pepper
- 1 (8-ounce) package precooked baby beets, diced
- 24 prepared crostini or toasted French bread slices
- ½ (10-ounce) log goat cheese, softened
- ⅓ cup chopped toasted pistachios
- Micro greens or chopped parsley

1. Combine oil, vinegar, honey, salt, and pepper in a bowl. Add beets and gently stir. Let stand for 15 minutes or cover and refrigerate until ready to serve.

2. Spread each crostini evenly with goat cheese. Remove beets from marinade with a small, slotted spoon and arrange over goat cheese. Sprinkle with nuts; top with micro greens or chopped parsley.

SMOKED SALMON BRUSCHETTA WITH ARUGULA PESTO

MAKES 12 TO 18 SERVINGS

24 to 36 slices toasted crostini
Arugula Pesto (recipe at right)
4 ounces hot smoked sockeye salmon

This elegant smoked salmon bruschetta gets its fresh twist from a peppery Arugula Pesto that comes together in minutes—also try it as a sandwich spread, tossed with pasta, or drizzled over grilled vegetables. Construct this simple appetizer with lettuce leaves or celery sticks if you're avoiding bread or gluten.

Spread each crostini evenly with Arugula Pesto. Top with smoked salmon.

Arugula Pesto: Combine **3 cups lightly packed arugula** (about 3 ounces), **1 garlic clove, 2 tablespoons toasted pine nuts,** and **½ cup grated Parmesan cheese** in a food processor; pulse to coarsely chop. Add **2 tablespoons extra-virgin olive oil** and **1 tablespoon lemon juice;** pulse to form a thick paste. Season with **⅛ teaspoon fine sea salt** and **⅛ teaspoon coarsely ground black pepper.** Makes 1 cup.

SMOKY CHEDDAR-PECAN CHEESE BALL

MAKES 12 SERVINGS

This recipe is a bold version of the party favorite. Rolled in a crunchy coating of toasted pecans and fresh herbs, this cheese ball is packed with flavor and makes a stunning centerpiece for any appetizer spread. Serve it with crackers, pretzels, or sliced apples for a mix of textures and tastes.

8 ounces cream cheese, softened
2 cups (8 ounces) sharp cheddar cheese, shredded
1 tablespoon whole or coarse-grain mustard
1 tablespoon maple syrup
½ teaspoon smoked paprika
¼ teaspoon garlic powder
¼ teaspoon ground cayenne pepper
½ cup toasted pecans, finely chopped
Crackers and flat pretzels

1. Combine cream cheese, cheddar, mustard, maple syrup, smoked paprika, garlic powder, and cayenne in a large bowl. Stir until well blended and smooth.

2. Transfer cheese mixture onto a piece of plastic wrap and shape into a ball. Wrap tightly and refrigerate for at least 1 hour or until firm.

3. Unwrap cheese ball and roll in pecans, pressing gently to coat all sides. Rewrap until ready to serve with crackers and flat pretzels.

CÓCTEL DE CAMARONES

MAKES 5 CUPS OR 10 TO 12 SERVINGS

½ cup diced white or red onion

1 cup tomato cocktail mixer such as Clamato or vegetable juice

¼ cup ketchup

½ teaspoon lime zest

3 tablespoons fresh lime juice

2 to 3 teaspoons hot sauce

¼ teaspoon fine sea salt

¼ teaspoon coarsely ground black pepper

1 pound small, cooked, peeled-and-deveined shrimp

2 ripe tomatoes, seeded and diced

2 small celery ribs, minced

1 small jalapeño, seeded and finely diced

½ seedless cucumber, diced

¼ cup chopped fresh cilantro

1 avocado, thinly sliced or chopped

This version of Mexican shrimp cocktail is a refreshing, fun dish that's perfect as an appetizer on a balmy day. Using precooked shrimp (preferably wild caught) makes it incredibly quick and easy to prepare—just mix, chill, and serve.

1. Combine onion and cold water to cover in a small bowl. Let stand for 15 minutes; drain and set aside.
2. Stir together tomato cocktail mixer, ketchup, lime zest and juice, hot sauce, salt, and pepper in a bowl.
3. Stir in reserved onion, shrimp, tomatoes, celery, jalapeño, cucumber, and cilantro. Cover and refrigerate for at least 30 minutes before serving to allow flavors to marry.
4. Spoon into serving cups and top with avocado.

CHILLED SHRIMP WITH TWO SAUCES

MAKES 6 SERVINGS

2 pounds cooked-and-deveined large shrimp, peeled, if desired
Spicy Rémoulade (recipe at right)
Quick Cocktail Sauce (recipe at right)
Lemon slices

Many grocery stores sell high-quality cooked frozen shrimp—just thaw and serve. Or, if your market offers steamed shrimp at the fish counter, take advantage of the convenience. Paired with a zesty homemade cocktail sauce and a bold, creamy rémoulade, this chilled shrimp platter is perfect for entertaining with minimal effort. Try the rémoulade as a dipping sauce for boiled or steamed artichokes or a sandwich spread—yum!

Arrange shrimp on a large serving platter. If serving on a hot day, mound shrimp over ice in a roasting pan or rimmed platter. Don't allow shrimp to soak in melted ice. Drain platter frequently, if necessary. Serve with Spicy Rémoulade, Quick Cocktail Sauce, and lemon slices.

Spicy Rémoulade: Combine ½ cup mayonnaise, 1 tablespoon whole-grain or Creole mustard, ¼ teaspoon lemon zest, 2 teaspoons fresh lemon juice, 2 teaspoons rinsed-and-drained capers, and ½ teaspoon Cajun or Creole seasoning in a bowl, stirring well. If desired, stir in **1 teaspoon chopped fresh tarragon.** Makes ⅔ cup.

Quick Cocktail Sauce: Combine ⅔ cup ketchup, ⅓ cup chili sauce, 2 tablespoons prepared horseradish, ½ teaspoon grated lemon zest, 1 teaspoon fresh lemon juice, and **1 teaspoon Worcestershire sauce** in a bowl, stirring well. Makes about 1¼ cups.

SUN-DRIED TOMATO-AND-PESTO TORTA

MAKES 12 TO 18 SERVINGS

This stunning appetizer layers rich, creamy flavors with vibrant Mediterranean ingredients. Best of all, there's no cooking involved—just simple layering and chilling for a beautifully marbled spread that's ideal for entertaining, bringing elegance to any gathering with a minimal amount of effort.

2 (8-ounce) packages cream cheese, softened
4 tablespoons salted butter, softened
¼ cup grated Parmesan cheese
2 teaspoons Italian seasoning blend
½ teaspoon coarsely ground black pepper
¼ teaspoon garlic powder
½ cup oil-packed sun-dried tomatoes, drained, finely chopped, and divided
½ cup prepared refrigerated basil pesto, divided
¼ cup toasted pine nuts, divided
Garnishes: toasted pine nuts, fresh rosemary sprigs
Crackers or sliced baguette slices

1. Line a 3- to 4-cup small bowl or ramekin with plastic wrap, leaving a few inches of overhang for easy removal.
2. Combine cream cheese, butter, Parmesan, Italian seasoning, pepper, and garlic powder in a large bowl, stirring until smooth and well blended.
3. Spread one-third of cream cheese mixture evenly into bottom of prepared bowl. Add half of sun-dried tomatoes and gently spread into an even layer. Add half of basil pesto, smoothing it over tomatoes. Sprinkle with half of pine nuts.
4. Spread with another one-third cream cheese mixture, remaining half of sun-dried tomatoes, remaining half of pesto, and remaining half of pine nuts. Finish with the last one-third of cream cheese mixture, smoothing the top.
5. Cover and refrigerate for at least 2 hours or until firm. When ready to serve, invert onto a serving plate, remove plastic wrap, and garnish, if desired. Serve with crackers or toasted baguette slices.

> Whether you're hosting a small group of close friends or your whole neighborhood garden club, this impressive appetizer is sure to please.

GOAT CHEESE-AND-PISTACHIO GRAPES

MAKES ABOUT 2 DOZEN

These adorable, bite-size appetizers are popular for any occasion—casual to upscale. Serve them chilled for a refreshing, savory-sweet treat that pairs beautifully with a glass of wine. You may get a couple more or less, depending on the size of the grapes. Make them hours ahead and add to a charcuterie board or serve on their own.

3 ounces goat cheese, softened

1 cup (about 24) small seedless grapes (red and/or green), washed and thoroughly dried

⅓ cup very finely chopped pistachios or another nut

1. Press about 1 teaspoon softened goat cheese around each grape, rolling and pressing until evenly coated.

2. Roll cheese-coated grapes in chopped pistachios, pressing lightly to adhere. Place on a plate and chill for at least 30 minutes or until firm.

SMOKY CHIPOTLE-BACON DEVILED EGGS

MAKES 1 DOZEN

Deviled eggs get a bold upgrade in this slightly spicy take on a favorite. A touch of chopped chipotle peppers in adobo sauce gives the creamy yolk filling a warm, smoky heat, while crispy bacon adds crunch and savory depth.

- 6 large hard-boiled eggs, peeled
- 3 tablespoons mayonnaise
- 2 tablespoons sour cream
- 1 tablespoon minced dill pickles, drained well
- 1 to 2 teaspoons finely chopped chipotle peppers in adobo sauce (to taste)
- ⅛ teaspoon smoked paprika (optional)
- ⅛ teaspoon fine sea salt
- 3 slices crisp cooked bacon, crumbled and divided
- Garnish: chopped fresh chives

1. Slice eggs in half lengthwise and transfer yolks to a large bowl. Mash yolks with a fork until smooth. Stir in mayonnaise; sour cream; pickles; chipotle peppers; smoked paprika, if desired; and salt. Stir until creamy and well blended. Fold in half of crumbled bacon.
2. Spoon or pipe filling into egg white halves. Sprinkle with remaining half of bacon and a light dusting of smoked paprika. Garnish, if desired. Keep chilled until ready to serve.

WEST INDIES CRAB SALAD

MAKES ABOUT 4 CUPS

- 1 small, sweet onion, finely chopped and divided
- 1 pound jumbo lump, lump, or backfin crab, drained and picked
- ½ cup vegetable oil
- ¼ cup apple cider or white vinegar
- ½ teaspoon fine sea salt
- ¼ teaspoon coarsely ground black pepper
- ½ cup ice water
- 1 tablespoon chopped fresh parsley
- Saltine crackers or lettuce leaves
- Garnish: fresh parsley sprigs

This cool, refreshing crab salad originated in Mobile, Alabama. It's traditionally made with sweet lump crabmeat marinated in a simple mixture of vinegar, oil, onion, and ice water, then chilled until the flavors meld. The result is light, tangy, and perfect for hot weather—often served over lettuce or with saltine crackers on the side. Tradition calls for fresh lump crab. Try backfin, claw, or pasteurized crab for a lower-cost way to enjoy this Gulf Coast favorite on any budget.

1. Spread half of chopped onion in bottom of a shallow dish. Gently layer crabmeat over onion. Top with remaining half of onion. Whisk together oil, vinegar, salt, and pepper in a bowl; drizzle oil mixture evenly over top. Pour ½ cup ice water evenly over salad.

2. Cover and refrigerate for at least 2 hours or overnight. Do not stir until ready to serve. Sprinkle with parsley. Serve with crackers or on lettuce leaves. Garnish, if desired.

SMOKED TROUT DIP

MAKES 1½ CUPS

This creamy smoked trout dip brings together big flavors. Finely minced celery adds a bit of crunch to contrast with the smooth base. It's perfect as a make-ahead appetizer—serve it with crackers, cucumber rounds, or pumpernickel bread.

6 ounces cream cheese, softened
½ cup sour cream
2 teaspoons prepared horseradish
⅛ teaspoon lemon zest
1 teaspoon lemon juice
1 celery rib, finely minced
1 tablespoon chopped fresh dill
⅛ teaspoon coarsely ground black pepper
4 ounces smoked trout, skin removed and flaked
Garnish: fresh dill sprigs

1. Combine cream cheese, sour cream, horseradish, and lemon zest and juice in a large bowl, stirring until smooth. Stir in celery, dill, and pepper. Fold in flaked smoked trout.

2. Cover and chill for at least 30 minutes to allow flavors to meld. Let come to room temperature before serving for best texture. Garnish, if desired.

SOUTHERN PICKLED SHRIMP

MAKES 4 CUPS

⅔ cup apple cider vinegar

½ cup extra-virgin olive oil

1 teaspoon celery seeds

1 teaspoon mustard seeds

½ teaspoon fine sea salt

½ teaspoon coarsely ground black pepper

½ teaspoon crushed red pepper flakes

1¼ pounds small or medium-size cooked shrimp, peeled and deveined*

1 Vidalia or other sweet onion, halved and thinly sliced

1 small red bell pepper, chopped

1 lemon or lime, halved and sliced

2 tablespoons capers, drained

2 small cloves garlic, thinly sliced

3 tablespoons chopped fresh parsley

> Make a satisfying meal out of this seafood-focused appetizer by serving it over warmed leftover rice. Add a simple lettuce-and-tomato salad, if you like. Both additions will complement, rather than compete, with the tangy shrimp.

Pickled shrimp is a classic Southern dish that's perfect for entertaining, whether served as an appetizer or spooned over a crisp green salad. This recipe combines sweet Vidalia onions, tart cider vinegar, and the briny bite of tiny capers, creating a well-balanced marinade that infuses the shrimp with bright-and-zesty flavors. It's best when made a day in advance, allowing the flavors to meld beautifully.

1. Whisk together vinegar, oil, celery seeds, mustard seeds, salt, black pepper, and red pepper flakes in a large bowl until well combined.

2. Add shrimp, onion, bell pepper, lemon slices, capers, and garlic. Cover and refrigerate for 8 to 24 hours, stirring occasionally.

3. Stir well and sprinkle with parsley just before serving.

* Many seafood counters will steam raw shrimp for you. The shells add weight, so buy about 2 pounds raw shrimp in the shell to get 1¼ pounds peeled and deveined.

BEVERAGES

40 Hibiscus Tea Lemonade
41 Watermelon Agua Fresca
42 Tropical Sangría
43 White Linen Cocktail
44 Tiki Blush
45 Frozen Gin and Tonic
46 Mocha Punch
47 Bushwhacker Shake
48 Limoncello Mojito
49 Whiskey Amaretto Slushie

HIBISCUS TEA LEMONADE

MAKES 6 CUPS

5 individual hibiscus tea bags
1½ cups boiling or hot water
1 cup granulated sugar
1 cup fresh lemon juice
3 cups cold water
Ice
Garnish: lemon slices

With its ruby hue and tart, floral flavor, hibiscus tea makes a refreshing take on a summer favorite. This homemade version involves steeping hibiscus tea bags and blending the brew with fresh-squeezed lemon juice and a touch of sweetener. It's light, bright, and just the thing for warm afternoons or any time you want a bold, thirst-quenching drink. Serve over ice with lemon slices, or add a sprig of mint for a pretty finish.

1. Steep tea bags in 1½ cups boiling water for about 5 to 7 minutes. Remove tea bags and add sugar, stirring until dissolved. Let cool.

2. Combine brewed hibiscus tea mixture and lemon juice in a 1-quart jar or pitcher. Stir in 3 cups cold water. Refrigerate until well chilled and ready to serve. Serve over ice. Garnish, if desired.

WATERMELON AGUA FRESCA

MAKES 6½ CUPS

8 cups cubed watermelon, chilled and divided
⅓ cup fresh lime juice, divided
¼ cup granulated sugar, divided
1 cup cold water, divided
Garnish: lime slices

This is a light, refreshing way to enjoy the natural sweetness of summer's favorite fruit. If you ever have leftover watermelon, store it in the freezer—it's perfect for recipes like this and helps chill the drink without extra ice. Since some watermelons are sweeter than others, taste as you go and adjust the lime juice and sugar to find the perfect balance. Serve ice-cold for the most refreshing sip on a warm day!

1. Place about half each of watermelon, lime juice, and sugar in a blender. Add ½ cup cold water. Blend until smooth, and transfer to a pitcher. Repeat with remaining half each of watermelon, juice, and sugar. Add remaining ½ cup cold water.

2. Strain mixture into a large bowl with a fine wire-mesh sieve to remove pulp. Transfer mixture to a pitcher. Serve over ice. Garnish, if desired.

TROPICAL SANGRÍA

MAKES ABOUT 5½ CUPS

2 tablespoons granulated sugar

2 tablespoons fresh lime or lemon juice

1 (750-milliliter) bottle Sauvignon Blanc, Pinot Grigio, or other white wine

1 cup orange-pineapple or orange juice

¾ cup passionfruit-, mango-, or other fruit-flavored vodka

¼ cup orange liqueur

2 kiwis, peeled and sliced

1 mango, peeled, pitted, and sliced

1 seedless orange, sliced and cut into wedges

1 cup fresh or frozen raspberries

Cracked ice

This drink captures the essence of summer in every sip. Crisp white wine is infused with an exotic blend of kiwi and mango—each lending a burst of color and juicy sweetness—while fresh raspberries add a tart, playful contrast. It's fruity, refreshing, and just the right kind of fancy for outdoor gatherings, brunches, or quiet porch moments. Let it chill for a bit so the flavors can mingle. On really hot days, pour it over ice and enjoy the cool tropical escape.

Combine sugar and lime juice in a 3-quart pitcher, stirring until sugar starts to dissolve. Stir in wine, juice, vodka, liqueur, kiwis, mango, orange, and raspberries. Cover and chill for at least 1 hour before serving over cracked ice.

WHITE LINEN COCKTAIL

MAKES 2 SERVINGS

1 ounce (2 tablespoons) fresh lemon juice

4 slices cucumber

3 ounces (about ⅓ cup) gin

2 ounces (¼ cup) St. Germain (elderflower liqueur)

1 ounce (2 tablespoons) Simple Syrup (recipe at right) or store-bought version

Ice

Sparkling water (optional)

Garnishes: cucumber ribbons, lemon slices

Light, crisp, and floral, this modern classic blends the botanical notes of gin with the delicate sweetness of elderflower liqueur. Fresh lemon juice and muddled cucumber add brightness and a cooling effect, making it an ideal sipper for spring and summer afternoons.

1. Combine lemon juice and cucumber slices in a cocktail shaker. Muddle until cucumber is crushed. Add gin, elderflower liqueur, and Simple Syrup.

2. Fill shaker with ice and shake until well chilled. Strain equally into 2 coupe glasses or 2 ice-filled highball glasses; top each with a splash of sparkling water, if desired. Garnish, if desired.

Simple Syrup: Combine **1 part granulated sugar** and **1 part warm water.** Let stand, stirring occasionally, until sugar dissolves. Store in the refrigerator for up to 1 week.

Variation: After running out of Simple Syrup and fresh lemons during a cocktail party, I grabbed some frozen lemonade concentrate and used 2 tablespoons per shaker. It was delicious and so easy!

TIKI BLUSH

MAKES ABOUT 10 CUPS

I developed a similar cocktail about 15 years ago when I was Food Editor at *Coastal Living* magazine. Besides being the happiest color pink, its ease of preparation and great flavor made it a hit with readers. I've since renamed it, as the coconut rum evokes a vintage tiki vibe. The original recipe didn't use sparkling water. Nowadays my taste has shifted to less-sweet beverages, so the spritz of bubbles lightens it and makes it even more refreshing.

---

1 (1.75-liter) bottle refrigerated raspberry lemonade

1½ cups coconut rum, chilled

1 cup amaretto or almond-flavored liqueur, chilled

Ice

Raspberry or lime sparkling water (optional)

Garnishes: fresh raspberries, lemon slices

Combine lemonade, rum, and liqueur in a large pitcher. Pour each serving into an ice-filled glass about ¾ full. Top off with sparkling water, if desired. Garnish, if desired.

FROZEN GIN AND TONIC

MAKES 2 TO 3 SERVINGS

¼ seedless cucumber, sliced*

½ cup gin

3 tablespoons granulated sugar or ¼ cup Simple Syrup (page 43)

½ teaspoon grated lime zest

¼ cup fresh lime juice

2½ cups crushed or cracked ice

½ cup cucumber, lime, or plain sparkling water or tonic water

2 dashes orange or other bitters (optional)

Lime slices

Blending fresh cucumber with gin, lime, and a touch of orange bitters creates a smooth, refreshing drink with a subtle citrus twist. Using cucumber or lime sparkling water enhances the fresh flavors, but regular tonic works just as well. Light, cooling, and slightly fizzy, it's an effortless way to elevate your next happy hour.

Combine cucumber, gin, sugar, lime zest and juice, and ice in a blender. Blend until smooth. Stir in sparkling water and, if desired, bitters. Pour into rocks glasses. Serve with lime slices.

*If using a regular or garden cucumber, peel first before blending, as the peel can add a bitter flavor to the drink.

MOCHA PUNCH

MAKES 10 CUPS

1 cup granulated sugar
⅓ cup instant coffee granules
¼ cup cocoa powder
1 cup hot water
1 tablespoon vanilla extract
1 (1½- or 2-quart) container chocolate ice cream
4 cups milk
Whipped cream
Garnish: cocoa powder

This nonalcoholic beverage is a hit anytime but especially on hot summer days. I will often serve it as dessert with a simple shortbread cookie. Using instant coffee rather than brewed coffee is important because the concentrated flavor is necessary. Use decaf if serving in the evening. Ice-cream packages seem to get smaller. In this recipe, I like to use a natural brand of ice cream that comes in a 1½-quart container, but opt for a half gallon (2 quarts) if you prefer.

1. Combine sugar, coffee, and cocoa in a bowl or pint jar. Add 1 cup water, stirring until sugar and coffee dissolve. Stir in vanilla. Cover and refrigerate until chilled.

2. Spoon ice cream into a punch or other large bowl. Add chilled coffee mixture and milk, whisking until somewhat smooth. Ladle into cups and top with whipped cream. Garnish, if desired.

BUSHWHACKER SHAKE

MAKES 5 CUPS

1 cup coconut cream

½ cup milk

2 ounces (¼ cup) coffee liqueur

2 ounces (¼ cup) crème de cacao

2 ounces (¼ cup) Irish cream liqueur

2 ounces (¼ cup) vanilla rum or dark rum

2 cups vanilla ice cream

2 tablespoons chocolate syrup

2 cups crushed ice

Garnish: finely grated chocolate

Creamy, boozy, and irresistibly decadent, this rich beverage is like a grown-up milkshake with a tropical twist. There are lots of variations, and you can mix and match liqueurs. Most use coconut cream, which is very sweet—similar to coconut-flavored sweetened condensed milk. I like using the less-sweet coconut cream instead because there's plenty of sweetness in the other ingredients. If you can't find it, you can use the thickened, creamy coconut mixture that rises to the top of regular-fat coconut milk.

Combine coconut cream, milk, liqueurs, rum, ice cream, syrup, and ice in a blender; process until smooth. Pour into glasses; garnish, if desired.

LIMONCELLO MOJITO

MAKES ABOUT 6 SERVINGS

½ cup fresh lemon juice
⅓ cup granulated sugar
½ cup fresh mint leaves
1 (750-milliliter) bottle limoncello liqueur, chilled
Sparkling water or club soda, chilled
Garnishes: fresh mint leaves, lemon slices

Limoncello is a sweet, intensely lemon-flavored Italian liqueur traditionally made from lemon zest, alcohol, sugar, and water. It pairs beautifully with fresh mint for a summery herbal twist. Add a splash of sparkling water to lighten the strength.

1. Combine lemon juice, sugar, and mint in a large, wide-mouth pitcher. Crush mint with a muddler or the back of a wooden spoon, stirring and mashing until sugar dissolves and mint is bruised. Stir in limoncello.

2. Fill rocks glasses with ice. Pour ⅓ to ½ cup limoncello mixture into each glass and top with a splash of sparking water. Garnish, if desired.

WHISKEY AMARETTO SLUSHIE

MAKES 6 CUPS

2 cups boiling or hot water

3 black tea bags

¾ cup granulated sugar

1 (12-ounce) container frozen lemonade concentrate, thawed

1 cup bourbon or rye whiskey

½ cup amaretto liqueur

Sparkling water or ginger ale (optional)

This riff on a bourbon slush combines the smooth depth of whiskey with the almondy sweetness of amaretto, balanced by citrusy lemonade. It freezes beautifully and scoops up into frosty perfection. It's like getting your favorite cocktail in snow-cone form!

1. Combine 2 cups boiling water and tea bags in a large bowl. Let tea bags steep for 3 to 5 minutes. Stir in sugar and let stand until sugar dissolves. Let cool to room temperature.

2. Stir in lemonade concentrate, bourbon, and amaretto. Pour into a freezer-safe container and freeze for at least 8 hours or overnight, until mostly solid (mixture will be icy and not completely frozen).

3. To serve, scrape into slushy portions and scoop into glasses. Top with a splash of sparkling water, if desired.

BREAKFAST

52 Creamy Kale-and-Cashew Smoothie
53 Brown Sugar-Cinnamon Overnight Oatmeal
54 Open-Faced Avocado-Egg Salad Sandwich
55 Smoked Salmon Breakfast Wrap
56 No-Bake Chocolate-Almond Breakfast Cookies

CREAMY KALE-AND-CASHEW SMOOTHIE

MAKES 4 CUPS

Blending kale with cashews and dates creates a naturally sweet-and-satisfying drink, while banana adds smoothness and fresh ginger brings a hint of warmth. Packed with fiber, healthy fats, and plant-based protein, it's both nourishing and refreshing.

- 1½ cups unsweetened vanilla almond milk (or any milk)
- 1 (3.5-ounce) bunch lacinato or other kale leaves, stems removed (about 1½ cups packed)
- ⅓ cup raw or toasted cashews
- 4 to 5 pitted Medjool dates
- 2 frozen bananas, cut into pieces
- ½ teaspoon freshly grated ginger
- 2 teaspoons vanilla extract
- 1 cup cracked ice

Combine almond milk, kale, cashews, dates, bananas, ginger, vanilla, and ice in a blender. Blend until smooth, adding more ice if needed. Serve immediately.

Variation: For a high-protein treat, add **2 scoops vanilla protein powder.** You may need to add about **½ cup additional almond milk** if mixture gets thick.

BROWN SUGAR–CINNAMON OVERNIGHT OATMEAL

MAKES 2 SERVINGS

1 cup old-fashioned oats

1 cup milk or vanilla unsweetened almond milk

2 tablespoons vanilla protein powder (optional)

1½ tablespoons light brown sugar

¾ teaspoon ground cinnamon

½ teaspoon vanilla extract

2 tablespoons toasted chopped pecans or walnuts (optional)

This easy, no-cook breakfast is creamy, lightly spiced, and packed with flavor. The cinnamon-infused oats soften overnight, creating a deliciously rich texture, while toasted pecans add the perfect crunch.

1. Combine oats; milk; protein powder, if desired; brown sugar; cinnamon; and vanilla in a large bowl. Divide between 2 (1-cup) jars or bowls. Cover and refrigerate overnight.

2. When ready to serve, stir oats until well blended. Sprinkle each serving evenly with pecans, if desired.

OPEN-FACED AVOCADO-EGG SALAD SANDWICH

MAKES 4 SERVINGS

1 ripe avocado, coarsely chopped

¼ teaspoon grated lemon zest

½ tablespoon fresh lemon juice

¼ teaspoon fine sea salt

¼ teaspoon coarsely ground black pepper

4 hard-boiled eggs, peeled and chopped

4 slices large heirloom tomato

4 slices sprouted wheat or whole wheat bread or toast

¼ cup packed baby arugula

2 tablespoons cooked-and-crumbled bacon (optional)

Creamy avocado adds richness to a simple egg salad, while peppery arugula and juicy heirloom tomatoes bring brightness and contrast. Simple yet flavorful, this sandwich is ideal for breakfast, lunch, or a light dinner. Add a sprinkle of bacon bits or crushed red pepper flakes for an extra kick. Serve on hearty rustic or seeded bread for extra fiber and nutrition. Unless you consider toasting bread "cooking," do so because the sandwich is more appealing and easier to eat when the bread is crisp.

1. Combine avocado, lemon zest and juice, salt, and pepper in a large bowl. Stir in chopped eggs.
2. Place a slice of tomato on each piece of bread or toast. Top evenly with arugula and egg mixture. Sprinkle with bacon, if desired.

SMOKED SALMON BREAKFAST WRAP

MAKES 2 SERVINGS

4 tablespoons whipped cream cheese

2 (8- to 10-inch) tortillas

2 teaspoons everything bagel seasoning

1 cup lightly packed baby spinach

4 ounces smoked sockeye salmon

½ small zucchini, thinly sliced into ribbons with a vegetable peeler

2 hard-boiled eggs, sliced (optional)

This tasty breakfast sandwich is a fresh, flavorful way to start your day with a balance of protein, healthy fats, and crisp veggies. Creamy whipped cream cheese pairs beautifully with smoky salmon, thin zucchini ribbons, and bright chives, all wrapped in a low-carb tortilla for a meal that's satisfying yet light. For more protein, add sliced hard-boiled eggs.

Spread cream cheese evenly over one side of each tortilla. Sprinkle evenly with bagel seasoning. Top with spinach, salmon, and zucchini ribbons. Place egg slices in center, if desired. Roll each tortilla tightly and cut in half.

NO-BAKE CHOCOLATE-ALMOND BREAKFAST COOKIES

MAKES ABOUT 2½ DOZEN

¾ cup no-sugar-added almond butter
⅓ cup honey
1 teaspoon vanilla extract
¼ to ½ teaspoon cinnamon
¼ teaspoon fine sea salt
3 tablespoons vanilla protein powder
3 tablespoons cocoa powder
1 cup quick oats (not old-fashioned)
¼ cup unsweetened shredded coconut
¼ cup mini dark-chocolate chips

> Take a few minutes on a Sunday afternoon to mix up a batch of these yummy bites for the fridge, and you'll have an easy start to your day throughout the week.

These no-bake cookies offer a satisfying mix of protein, fiber, and natural sweetness. Best of all, they can be stored in the refrigerator for up to 2 weeks or in the freezer for up to 2 months!

1. Combine almond butter, honey, and vanilla in a large bowl, stirring until smooth. Stir in cinnamon and salt. Stir in protein powder and cocoa powder. Stir in oats, coconut, and chocolate chips.

2. Scoop about 1½ to 2 tablespoons dough into a ball and press into cookie-shaped patties. Cover and chill until ready to serve.

SANDWICHES and WRAPS

- **60** Dilled Egg Salad
- **61** Pimiento Cheese
- **62** Elevated Cream Cheese-and-Olive Sandwiches
- **63** Ham Salad
- **64** Turkey with Rosemary-Orange Marmalade Sauce
- **65** Bahn Mi Sandwiches
- **66** Lemony Lobster Rolls
- **67** Chicken, Prosciutto, and Goat Cheese Sandwiches
- **68** Mediterranean Hummus Wrap with Vinaigrette
- **69** Greek Chicken-and-Zucchini Wrap
- **70** No-Cook Chicken (Larb) Salad Wraps
- **72** Veggie Summer Rolls with Hoisin Peanut Sauce
- **73** Spicy Lentil Lettuce Wraps
- **74** Chicken-and-Black Bean Tostadas

DILLED EGG SALAD

MAKES 3½ CUPS

⅓ cup mayonnaise

2 tablespoons sour cream

1 teaspoon Dijon mustard

2 teaspoons fresh dill, minced

½ teaspoon fine sea salt

¼ coarsely ground black pepper

2 small celery ribs, finely chopped

1 green onion, finely sliced

12 hard-boiled eggs, peeled

Garnish: fresh parsley sprigs

Creamy, flavorful, and endlessly customizable, this sandwich filling offers all the great taste of deviled eggs in a simple, scoopable format. A blend of mayonnaise and a touch of sour cream gives it a rich-but-balanced texture, while a hint of mustard adds zip. Chopping the egg yolks separately helps ensure a smooth, velvety base without large chunks, allowing you to fold in the firmer egg whites for added texture.

1. Combine mayonnaise, sour cream, mustard, dill, salt, and pepper in a large bowl. Stir in celery and onion.

2. Cut eggs in half and chop whites and yolks separately. Stir whites and yolks into mayonnaise mixture. Serve as is, over greens, or as a sandwich spread. Garnish, if desired.

PIMIENTO CHEESE

MAKES 3½ CUPS

- 2 (8-ounce) packages sharp cheddar cheese
- 4 ounces cream cheese or Neufchatel, softened
- ⅔ cup mayonnaise
- ½ teaspoon grated onion (optional)
- 2 teaspoons Worcestershire sauce
- ½ teaspoon hot sauce
- ¼ teaspoon coarsely ground black pepper
- 1 (4-ounce) jar chopped pimientos, drained, or 1 roasted red bell pepper, diced

Pimiento cheese is a Southern classic that works double duty—as a rich sandwich spread or a bold topper for fresh greens. It's incredibly easy to whip up—especially in a food processor—for a smooth, creamy texture. For a chunkier version with more bite, simply stir the ingredients together by hand after shredding the cheese. A 4-ounce jar of chopped pimientos will do the trick, but I often reach for roasted red bell peppers instead—I always have a few on hand and love the subtle smoky flavor they add. For a variation, you can substitute a brick of Colby, Monterey Jack, or pepper-Jack cheese for half of the cheddar.

1. Shred cheddar cheese with a box grater or in a food processor. Set aside.
2. Combine cream cheese; mayonnaise; onion, if desired; Worcestershire; hot sauce; and black pepper in a food processor fitted with a blade or in a mixing bowl. Process or beat until smooth and well blended.
3. Add reserved cheddar; process or beat until well blended. Stir in pimientos.

ELEVATED CREAM CHEESE-AND-OLIVE SANDWICHES

MAKES 4 SANDWICHES OR 1⅓ CUPS

1 (8-ounce) package cream cheese, softened
2 teaspoons finely chopped fresh or ¾ teaspoon dried dill
¼ teaspoon lemon zest
⅛ teaspoon coarsely ground black pepper
⅔ cup finely chopped pimiento-stuffed green olives
2 teaspoons finely minced shallot
8 slices olive, rosemary-sea salt, sourdough, or rye bread, toasted, if desired
Butter lettuce or arugula leaves (optional)
Thin cucumber slices (optional)

Growing up, basic cream cheese-and-olive sandwiches on white bread—no crusts!—were in my beloved metal lunchbox almost every day. This elevated take on the classic is salty, creamy, and satisfyingly nostalgic—but with a grown-up twist. Briny green olives are finely chopped and folded into whipped cream cheese, along with shallots, lemon zest, and fresh herbs for added depth. The best sandwiches are made with fresh bakery or deli bread—use your favorite. I keep the spread in a container and make sandwiches as I want them or simply use it as a dip on top of sturdy crackers.

1. Beat cream cheese, dill, lemon zest, and pepper with an electric mixer until creamy and light. Stir in olives and shallot.

2. Spread cream cheese mixture evenly on 4 bread slices. Layer evenly with lettuce and cucumber, if desired, and place remaining 4 bread slices on top. Cut into halves or quarters.

HAM SALAD

MAKES 3 CUPS

⅓ cup mayonnaise
1 tablespoon chopped onion
1 teaspoon dry mustard
¼ teaspoon coarsely ground black pepper
¾ pound fully cooked baked or smoked ham, cut into pieces
¼ cup chopped pickles
2 small celery ribs, chopped
Pretzel buns

Ham salad is a versatile, economical way to use up leftover ham, transforming it into a creamy, flavorful spread perfect for sandwiches or crackers. It's especially delicious when piled onto a soft pretzel roll, where the salty-sweet combination shines. For extra flavor, spread the bread with a bit of Honey-Mustard Dressing (page 124) before adding the filling.

Combine mayonnaise, onion, mustard, and pepper in a food processor. Pulse until blended. Add ham and process until mixture is finely chopped and well blended. Add pickles and celery; pulse until blended. Serve on pretzel buns.

TURKEY WITH ROSEMARY-ORANGE MARMALADE SAUCE

MAKES 4 SERVINGS

A simple deli turkey sandwich gets an elegant upgrade with this sweet-and-savory spread made from orange marmalade and fresh rosemary. Serve it on your favorite sandwich bread—croissants are delicious, but rosemary-sourdough bread from the deli is another superb option.

⅓ cup mayonnaise
2 tablespoons orange marmalade
1 teaspoon minced fresh rosemary
⅛ teaspoon fine sea salt
⅛ teaspoon coarsely ground black pepper
4 large croissants, split
1 cup very loosely packed arugula
1 ripe tomato, thinly sliced
¾ pound sliced roasted or smoked turkey

1. Combine mayonnaise, marmalade, rosemary, salt, and pepper in a small bowl.
2. Spread cut sides of croissants with marmalade mixture. Layer bottom halves evenly with arugula, tomato slices, and turkey. Add top halves of bread.

BAHN MI SANDWICHES

MAKES 4 SERVINGS

⅓ cup plain rice vinegar

2 tablespoons water

2 tablespoons granulated sugar

⅛ teaspoon fine sea salt

½ cup julienned or shredded daikon radish or jicama

¼ cup slivered white onion

1 carrot, julienned or shredded

½ red bell pepper, julienned or thinly sliced into strips

¼ cup mayonnaise

2 teaspoons sriracha sauce

1 French baguette, cut into 4 (4-inch) pieces

12 ounces thinly sliced lean roast beef (from the deli)

½ English cucumber, sliced

Fresh cilantro leaves

These Vietnamese-style sandwiches use thinly sliced deli roast beef for a quick-and-flavorful twist on the classic banh mi. A simple slaw made with pickled daikon or jicama, carrots, and red bell pepper adds crunch and brightness, while a creamy sriracha mayo gives just the right amount of heat. If you can't find daikon or jicama, just use more carrot or bell pepper. Use soft French rolls or sections of baguette with a crisp crust and fluffy interior—perfect for holding all the juicy, savory, and tangy layers.

1. Combine vinegar, 2 tablespoons water, sugar, and salt in a large bowl; stir until sugar dissolves. Stir in daikon, onion, carrot, and bell pepper. Cover and refrigerate for 30 minutes to 24 hours, stirring occasionally.

2. Combine mayonnaise and sriracha sauce in a small bowl. Slice each bread section in half lengthwise and scoop out some of the soft interior (discard or save for other uses). Spread inside of bread evenly with mayonnaise mixture. Layer bottom halves evenly with roast beef and cucumber. Drain vegetable mixture and place evenly over beef; top with cilantro leaves and top halves of bread.

LEMONY LOBSTER ROLLS

MAKES 2 SERVINGS

Lobster rolls are a summer staple in New England, featuring tender, sweet lobster meat tossed in a light dressing and served in unique "top-loading" hot dog buns. If you're looking for a more affordable option, look for frozen cooked langostinos or small shrimp. They make a fantastic substitute while still delivering a fresh, briny flavor.

8 ounces cooked lobster
¼ cup mayonnaise
1 celery rib, minced
¼ teaspoon lemon zest
2 teaspoons fresh lemon juice
1 teaspoon finely chopped chives or parsley
⅛ teaspoon fine sea salt
¼ teaspoon hot sauce
2 hot dog buns or croissants, split

Remove lobster meat from shells and evenly chop. Combine lobster, mayonnaise, celery, lemon zest and juice, chives, salt, and hot sauce in a medium-size bowl, stirring until well blended. Fill buns evenly with lobster mixture.

CHICKEN, PROSCIUTTO, AND GOAT CHEESE SANDWICHES

MAKES 4 SERVINGS

4 (5-inch) brioche, sourdough, or French bread rolls, split

½ cup soft goat cheese

2 roasted red bell peppers, cut into pieces

3 cups grilled-and-sliced or shredded cooked chicken

4 slices prosciutto

1 cup lightly packed arugula

½ cup refrigerated prepared pesto or 12 large fresh basil leaves

This savory, sophisticated sandwich layers grilled chicken, salty prosciutto, tangy goat cheese, and sweet roasted red bell peppers in a hearty brioche bun. A touch of pesto—or fresh basil leaves for a brighter bite—brings everything together. You can also substitute Arugula Pesto (page 26) and skip the fresh greens.

Spread bottom halves of rolls evenly with goat cheese (about 2 tablespoons per roll). Layer evenly with bell peppers, chicken, prosciutto, and arugula. Spread cut sides of top halves of rolls with pesto (about 2 tablespoons per roll) and place on top of arugula.

MEDITERRANEAN HUMMUS WRAP WITH VINAIGRETTE

MAKES 2 SERVINGS

2 (10- to 12-inch) flour tortillas
½ cup hummus (classic or roasted garlic)
8 large leaves of romaine or green leaf lettuce
1 tomato, sliced
½ seedless cucumber, sliced into strips
½ roasted red bell pepper, sliced into strips
2 very thin slices red onion
1 tablespoon pepperoncini rings
8 black or Kalamata olives, sliced
Basic Red Wine Vinaigrette (recipe at right)

This fresh, vibrant wrap is packed with Mediterranean flavors and finished with a bright vinaigrette. I like using the lower carb veggie wraps that are sold in various flavors (and pretty colors!). You can substitute a traditional flour tortilla, but even then, a flavored one (like chili) adds to the sandwich.

1. Place tortillas on a flat surface. Spread each evenly with ¼ cup hummus. Layer lettuce, tomato, cucumber, roasted bell pepper, and red onion on top. Top with pepperoncini and olives.

2. Drizzle desired amount of Basic Red Wine Vinaigrette over filling (not too much or sandwiches will get soggy). Roll up sandwiches. To help keep sandwiches securely rolled, place wrap diagonally at bottom of a large piece of parchment paper. Roll sandwich once to cover, then fold in sides of paper and continue to roll. Slice in half just before serving.

Basic Red Wine Vinaigrette: Combine ¼ cup extra-virgin olive oil, 2 tablespoons red wine vinegar, 1 tablespoon water, 2 teaspoons lemon juice, ½ teaspoon stone-ground or Dijon mustard, 1 teaspoon dried oregano, ¼ teaspoon garlic powder, ¼ teaspoon fine sea salt, and ⅛ teaspoon coarsely ground black pepper in a jar or small bowl. Cover with lid and shake until well blended. Makes ½ cup.

GREEK CHICKEN-AND-ZUCCHINI WRAP

MAKES 2 SERVINGS

This simple sandwich is a flavorful way to use up precooked chicken for an easy lunch or light dinner. Crisp zucchini, creamy hummus, tangy feta, and roasted red bell peppers come together with chicken and fresh spinach, all wrapped in a soft tortilla. It's a perfect no-cook meal for busy days, offering a balance of protein, veggies, and bold Mediterranean flavors.

1½ cups shredded rotisserie or sliced grilled chicken breast

½ cup crumbled feta cheese

1 tablespoon extra-virgin olive oil

2 teaspoons chopped fresh oregano

½ teaspoon lemon-pepper seasoning blend

1 small zucchini

½ cup Roasted Red Pepper Hummus (page 17) or store-bought version

2 (10-inch) multigrain soft wraps or whole wheat flour tortillas

1 cup lightly packed spinach or arugula leaves

1 roasted red bell pepper, drained and sliced into strips

1. Stir together chicken, feta, oil, oregano, and lemon-pepper seasoning in a large bowl. Set aside.

2. Slice ends from zucchini and cut lengthwise into thin ribbons using a vegetable peeler or mandolin. (Do not slice center containing seeds.)

3. Spread ¼ cup Roasted Red Pepper Hummus on one side of each tortilla. Layer spinach and zucchini evenly over hummus. Layer reserved chicken mixture and red bell pepper evenly over zucchini. Roll tightly; cover in plastic wrap and refrigerate until ready to serve.

NO-COOK CHICKEN (LARB) SALAD WRAPS

MAKES 6 SERVINGS

1 small garlic clove, minced

½ jalapeño, seeded and minced

1 teaspoon granulated sugar

1 teaspoon grated lime zest

3 tablespoons lime juice

2 tablespoons fish sauce

2 teaspoons soy sauce

1½ teaspoons toasted sesame oil

3 cups minced or shredded cooked chicken (rotisserie or leftover)

2 small carrots, julienned

1 small red bell pepper, julienned

½ red onion, thinly sliced

⅓ cup fresh cilantro

⅓ cup fresh mint leaves, torn

⅓ cup fresh Thai basil or regular basil leaves, torn

1 head romaine or butter lettuce, leaves separated

¼ cup chopped roasted peanuts or cashews

> Whether you're avoiding bread or just looking for a light, refreshing lunch, these wraps will hit the spot.

This colorful Thai-inspired dish combines fresh herbs, tangy lime, and savory seasonings. Authentic larb is served warm using ground meat, but this no-cook version makes it even easier by using precooked rotisserie or leftover chicken. Wrapped in crisp lettuce leaves, this light-yet-satisfying meal comes together in minutes—perfect for busy weeknights or a quick lunch.

1. Whisk together garlic, jalapeño, sugar, lime zest and juice, fish sauce, soy sauce, and sesame oil in a large bowl. Add chicken, carrots, and bell pepper, tossing to coat. Stir in onion, cilantro, mint, and basil.

2. Arrange lettuce leaves on a platter. Spoon chicken mixture into lettuce leaves. Sprinkle with nuts.

VEGGIE SUMMER ROLLS WITH HOISIN PEANUT SAUCE

MAKES 8 TO 10 ROLLS

3 ounces cellophane noodles

8 rice paper wrappers, divided

1 head green or red leaf lettuce

1 (7-ounce) package teriyaki-flavored or other baked tofu, sliced ¼-inch thick

1 carrot, julienned or grated

1 small seedless cucumber, julienned or grated

¼ cup lightly packed fresh cilantro leaves

¼ cup lightly packed fresh mint leaves

Hoisin-Peanut Dipping Sauce (recipe at right)

For best results, arrange noodles, lettuce, tofu slices, cucumbers, carrots, and herbs in small piles on a platter or cutting board. Dividing the mixture will ensure that you don't run out of any one ingredient before assembling all the rolls. Don't let the rice paper wrapper sit in the water too long and get too soft; it will tear while rolling. Tuck pointed ends of carrots or lettuce stems in the middle of the roll; otherwise, they may poke through the wrapper. The first few are usually loose and awkward. There is enough of the raw ingredients to make a couple of small practice rolls before you prepare any to serve to company.

1. Soak cellophane noodles in warm water for 10 minutes or until soft and pliable. Drain just before assembling.

2. Fill a shallow dish with warm water. Dip one rice paper wrapper into water and let soften for about 5 seconds or until just starting to become pliable. Repeat with remaining 7 wrappers.

3. Place wrappers on a flat surface and top evenly with noodles, lettuce, tofu, carrot, cucumber, cilantro, and mint. Fold bottom of each wrapper up over filling and roll one time. Fold sides of each wrapper inwards, then tightly roll wrapper from the bottom, enclosing filling. Repeat with remaining wrappers and filling.

4. Arrange on a serving platter and serve with Hoisin-Peanut Dipping Sauce.

Hoisin-Peanut Dipping Sauce: Combine ⅓ cup hoisin sauce, 2 tablespoons peanut butter, 2 tablespoons water, 1 tablespoon soy sauce, 1 tablespoon rice vinegar, and **1 teaspoon sriracha sauce** in a small bowl, whisking until smooth. Makes ⅔ cup.

SPICY LENTIL LETTUCE WRAPS

MAKES 3 TO 4 SERVINGS

3 tablespoons low-sodium soy sauce

2 tablespoons fresh lime juice

2 tablespoons hoisin sauce or light brown sugar

2 to 3 teaspoons sriracha or chili-garlic sauce

2 cups cooked lentils, black beans, or meatless crumbles

2 medium-size carrots, shredded or julienned

1 red bell pepper, cut into thin strips

9 to 12 Bibb lettuce leaves

¼ cup lightly packed fresh cilantro leaves

2 tablespoons chopped fresh mint

Lettuce wraps are often made with cooked ground beef. If you're looking for a ready-to-use alternative, there are plenty of convenient options available at the grocery store. Plant-based crumbles offer a similar texture and can be used straight from the package. For a hearty, protein-packed swap, canned lentils, black beans, or chickpeas work well. Tofu crumbles, or tempeh, add versatility and flavor without extra prep. If you prefer a meaty substitute, finely chopped deli roast beef or shredded rotisserie chicken can stand in for ground beef in wraps, salads, and more.

1. Combine soy sauce, lime juice, hoisin sauce, and sriracha sauce in a bowl. Add lentils, carrots, and bell pepper, tossing to coat.

2. Fill lettuce leaves with vegetable mixture. Top with cilantro and mint.

CHICKEN-AND-BLACK BEAN TOSTADAS

MAKES 4 TO 6 SERVINGS

- 1 cup sour cream
- 2 tablespoons chopped chipotle peppers in adobo sauce
- ½ teaspoon fine sea salt
- ½ teaspoon ground cumin
- ½ teaspoon grated lime zest
- 1 tablespoon lime juice
- 12 prepared crispy tostadas
- 3 cups chopped or shredded rotisserie chicken
- ¾ cup canned black beans, drained
- 1 cup yellow and red grape tomatoes, quartered or halved
- 2 avocados, sliced
- ½ cup fresh cilantro leaves
- Lime wedges

Turn rotisserie chicken into a quick, satisfying meal. A sauce of creamy chipotle peppers, sour cream, and cumin adds smoky heat, complementing the tender chicken and hearty black beans. Fresh avocado and juicy grape tomatoes provide the balance and brightness, while crispy tostada shells bring the perfect crunch. This no-fuss dish is great for busy weeknights and can be customized with your favorite garnishes, like crumbled queso fresco or a squeeze of lime.

Combine sour cream, chipotle peppers, salt, cumin, and lime zest and juice in a small bowl. Spread about 1½ tablespoons on each tostada. Sprinkle evenly with chicken, black beans, tomatoes, avocado, and cilantro. Serve with lime wedges.

SOUPS

78 Spicy Garden Veggie Soup
79 Chilled Cucumber Soup
80 Chilled Avocado Soup
81 Golden Tomato-and-Peach Gazpacho
82 All-the-Red-Things Chilled Soup
(Tomato-Watermelon-Berry Gazpacho)
84 Chilled Zucchini-and-Basil Soup
85 White Gazpacho with Cucumber
(Ajo Blanco Verde)

SPICY GARDEN VEGGIE SOUP

MAKES 8 CUPS

2 cups vegetable juice (plain or spicy)

¼ cup fresh lemon juice

2 tablespoons Worcestershire sauce

2 tablespoons prepared horseradish

2 tablespoons extra-virgin olive oil

2 pounds heirloom or beefsteak tomatoes, coarsely chopped

¼ red onion, chopped

½ cup packed cilantro leaves

2 garlic cloves, coarsely chopped

2 teaspoons fine sea salt

¾ teaspoon coarsely ground black pepper

1 jalapeño, seeded and minced (optional)

1 yellow bell pepper, chopped

1 zucchini, chopped

1 small cucumber, seeded and chopped

Garnish: fresh cilantro leaves

This cheery chilled soup is a refreshing way to use up an abundance of summer veggies from the garden. Blended with vegetable juice and bright, fresh produce, the dish is crisp, cooling, and just spicy enough, depending on the type of juice and the amount of jalapeño you choose to add. Serve it as a light lunch or starter on a hot day when turning on the stove is out of the question.

1. Combine vegetable juice, lemon juice, Worcestershire, horseradish, oil, tomatoes, red onion, cilantro, garlic, salt, and pepper in a food processor. Process until mixture is finely chopped. Transfer to a bowl.

2. Stir in jalapeño, if desired; bell pepper; zucchini; and cucumber. Cover and chill for several hours or overnight. Garnish, if desired.

CHILLED CUCUMBER SOUP

MAKES 5 CUPS

Cool, creamy, and packed with fresh herbs, this chilled soup is a perfect way to beat the summer heat. Whole yogurt adds tang and richness, blending smoothly with crisp cucumbers and a mix of tarragon, dill, and parsley. A splash of lemon juice lifts the flavors, making each spoonful bright and refreshing.

- 2 seedless cucumbers or 3 regular cucumbers, peeled, seeded, and coarsely chopped
- 2 teaspoons kosher salt
- 1 (16-ounce) container plain yogurt
- ⅓ cup fresh parsley leaves
- 3 green onions, coarsely chopped
- 3 tablespoons fresh dill
- 2 tablespoons fresh tarragon
- 2 tablespoons lemon juice
- Garnish: chopped fresh chives

1. Sprinkle cucumber with salt and transfer to a colander placed over a bowl. Let stand for 30 minutes, stirring occasionally.
2. Drain cucumber, discarding liquid. Combine cucumber, yogurt, parsley, green onions, dill, tarragon, and lemon juice in a blender. Blend until smooth.
3. Transfer to a bowl, if desired. Cover and chill for at least 1 hour before serving. Garnish, if desired.

CHILLED AVOCADO SOUP

MAKES ABOUT 4 CUPS

- 3 avocados, pitted and cut into pieces
- 2½ cups chicken or vegetable broth
- 2 tablespoons fresh lemon or lime juice
- ¾ teaspoon ground cumin
- ¾ teaspoon fine sea salt
- ⅛ teaspoon cayenne pepper
- ¼ cup fresh cilantro leaves
- Garnishes: fresh cilantro leaves, minced red bell pepper

Silky, refreshing, and full of bright flavors, this chilled dish is the perfect antidote to a hot day. The creamy richness of ripe avocados is balanced with a touch of citrus, warm cumin, and a hint of spice. It's an effortless make-ahead dish, ideal for serving as an elegant appetizer or a light summer lunch. A sprinkle of fresh cilantro adds a final burst of herbal freshness.

Combine avocado, broth, juice, cumin, salt, and cayenne pepper in a blender. Blend until smooth. Add cilantro and blend until cilantro is very finely chopped and mixture is smooth. Add additional broth or water if mixture is too thick. Garnish, if desired.

GOLDEN TOMATO-AND-PEACH GAZPACHO

MAKES ABOUT 7 CUPS

4 large yellow or orange tomatoes (about 2 pounds), cored, seeded, chopped, and divided
2 ripe peaches, peeled, pitted, chopped, and divided
1 small yellow bell pepper, chopped and divided
½ large cucumber, peeled, seeded, chopped, and divided
1 small garlic clove, minced and divided
¼ cup fresh basil leaves, divided
3 tablespoons sherry vinegar, divided
3 tablespoons extra-virgin olive oil, divided
1 teaspoon fine sea salt, divided
¼ teaspoon coarsely ground black pepper, divided
Garnishes: fresh basil sprigs, minced cucumber

On a hot day, sweet peaches blend harmoniously with juicy yellow or orange tomatoes. A splash of sherry vinegar adds the right amount of acidity. Since the sweetness and acidity of peaches and tomatoes can vary widely, taste the soup just before serving, adding more salt or vinegar, as desired.

1. Combine half each of tomatoes, peaches, bell pepper, cucumber, garlic, basil, vinegar, oil, salt, and black pepper in a food processor or blender. Blend until smooth. Pour into a bowl.
2. Repeat with remaining half of tomatoes, peaches, bell pepper, cucumber, garlic, basil, vinegar, oil, salt, and black pepper. Taste, then add more salt and pepper, if desired.
3. Transfer to a bowl; cover and refrigerate for at least 1 hour before serving. Garnish, if desired.

ALL-THE-RED-THINGS CHILLED SOUP (TOMATO-WATERMELON-BERRY GAZPACHO)

MAKES 6 CUPS

- 2 ripe tomatoes, seeded and chopped
- 2 packaged roasted baby beets, coarsely chopped
- 1 roasted red bell pepper, seeded and coarsely chopped
- ½ seedless cucumber, peeled and chopped
- ½ jalapeño or other mild pepper, seeded and chopped
- 4 cups cubed seedless watermelon
- 1 cup sliced strawberries
- 2 tablespoons chopped red onion
- 1 tablespoon chopped fresh basil
- 3 tablespoons red wine vinegar
- 1 tablespoon extra-virgin olive oil
- 2 teaspoons fine sea salt
- ¼ teaspoon coarsely ground black pepper
- Garnishes: chopped fresh chives, chopped cucumber, fresh basil sprigs

This vibrant chilled soup, featuring "all the red things," is simply bursting with color and flavor.

The genesis of this soup began with a tomato-watermelon mixture that eventually became the quirky-yet-delicious recipe below. It is the result of utilizing random leftover items in my fridge, but I enjoy the way they blend together. Sweet, juicy watermelon and plump strawberries add a sweet touch to a chilled tomato soup. The roasted red bell pepper and roasted beet offer loads of savory nutrition. I will tweak the vinegar each time I make the soup because the acidity in tomatoes can vary—use about half, taste the soup, then add more, if desired.

1. Combine tomatoes, beets, bell pepper, cucumber, jalapeño, watermelon, strawberries, red onion, basil, vinegar, oil, salt, and pepper in a blender or food processor. Blend until smooth. Cover and chill for 2 to 4 hours so flavors blend.
2. Pour into cups or bowls and garnish, if desired.

CHILLED ZUCCHINI-AND-BASIL SOUP

MAKES 4½ CUPS

1½ pounds zucchini, quartered and sliced
½ cup vegetable broth
¼ cup extra-virgin olive oil
¼ cup fresh basil leaves
1 tablespoon white balsamic vinegar
3 green onions, chopped
1 garlic clove, chopped
Garnishes: sliced green onions, chopped radish

This is a quick, refreshing way to use up an abundance of garden zucchini. With just a handful of ingredients and less than 10 minutes of prep, it's a simple, flavorful dish that's perfect for warm days. Fresh basil adds a bright, herbaceous note, while the zucchini blends into a silky-smooth texture. Serve it cold for a light appetizer or pair it with a salad for an easy meal on a hot summer night.

1. Combine zucchini, broth, oil, basil, vinegar, green onions, and garlic in a blender. Pulse or blend until smooth. Cover and chill until ready to serve.

2. Pour into small bowls or cups and garnish, if desired.

WHITE GAZPACHO WITH CUCUMBER (AJO BLANCO VERDE)

MAKES 4 CUPS

2 cups day-old white bread, crusts removed and torn into pieces

1½ cups cold water, divided

½ cup blanched almonds (or slivered almonds)

¼ shallot, coarsely chopped

1 seedless cucumber, peeled and chopped

2 cups seedless green grapes

2 tablespoons sherry vinegar or white wine vinegar

¼ cup extra-virgin olive oil, plus more for drizzling

½ teaspoon fine sea salt

Garnishes: extra-virgin olive oil, sliced grapes

This version of white gazpacho blends crisp cucumber into the traditional mix of grapes, almonds, garlic, and soaked bread for an extra layer of cooling refreshment. The result is a silky, pale-green soup that's perfect for warm weather—light, elegant, and packed with flavor. Serve it as a first course or pour into small glasses for a chic summer appetizer.

1. Soak bread in ½ cup water for 10 minutes.
2. Place almonds in a blender; puree until finely ground. Add shallot, cucumber, grapes, vinegar, oil, soaked bread and liquid, salt, and remaining 1 cup cold water. Blend until very smooth, adding more water, if needed, to adjust consistency.
3. Strain through a fine wire-mesh sieve for an extra-smooth soup. Chill for at least 2 hours before serving. Garnish, if desired.

SALADS and SIDES

88 Tomato Salad with Herbed Buttermilk Dressing
89 Marinated Heirloom Tomatoes with Burrata
90 Tomato-and-Avocado Salad
91 Wedge Salad with Buttermilk-Blue Cheese Dressing
92 Cantaloupe-and-Blueberry Salad with Honey, Lime, and Mint
93 Creamy Cucumber-and-Sweet Onion Salad
94 Celery Salad with Dates, Walnuts, and Parmesan
95 Marinated Celery-and-Chickpea Salad with Lemon-Shallot Vinaigrette
96 Cauliflower Chickpea Salad Bowl with Curry-Tahini Dressing
97 Hearts of Palm, Grapefruit, and Avocado Salad
98 Couscous-Tabbouleh Salad
99 Mediterranean White Bean Salad
100 Heirloom Tomato Panzanella with Brie and Basil
102 Moroccan Kale-and-Grain Salad with Cumin-Coriander Vinaigrette
103 Strawberry-Spinach Salad with Toasted Pecans and Honey-Poppy Seed Dressing
104 Chopped Salad with Avocado-Ranch Dressing
105 Simple Side Salad with Blended Ginger Dressing
106 Kale Salad with Orange-Sesame Dressing
107 Bibb Salad with Raspberries, Mango, Hazelnuts, Goat Cheese, and Raspberry Vinaigrette
108 Beet, Orange, and Blue Cheese Salad with Tarragon Vinaigrette
109 Simple Beet-and-Arugula Salad with Whipped Ricotta and Honey Vinaigrette
110 Carrot, Mango, and Jicama Slaw
111 Tex-Mex Coleslaw with Creamy Lime-Chipotle Dressing
112 Ramen Noodle Slaw

TOMATO SALAD WITH HERBED BUTTERMILK DRESSING

MAKES 4 SERVINGS

Buttermilk creates a perfect base for an herb-flecked salad dressing. Juicy heirloom tomatoes are the star of the show. With their rich aroma and natural balance of sweetness and acidity, they need little more to stand out.

2 pounds ripe, mixed heirloom tomatoes, sliced

Herbed Buttermilk Dressing (recipe at right)

Chopped fresh herbs such as basil, chives, and parsley

Coarsely ground black pepper

Garnish: fresh basil leaves

Arrange tomatoes on a platter or individual salad plates. Drizzle with Herbed Buttermilk Dressing. Sprinkle with basil and pepper. Garnish, if desired. Serve with additional dressing.

HERBED BUTTERMILK DRESSING

½ cup buttermilk

⅓ cup mayonnaise

⅓ cup sour cream

2 tablespoons apple cider vinegar

3 tablespoons chopped fresh basil, thyme, or chives

½ teaspoon fine sea salt

½ teaspoon coarsely ground black pepper

¼ teaspoon minced fresh garlic

Combine buttermilk, mayonnaise, sour cream, vinegar, basil, salt, pepper, and garlic in a bowl, whisking until smooth. Cover and chill until ready to serve. Makes 1⅓ cups.

MARINATED HEIRLOOM TOMATOES WITH BURRATA

MAKES 4 SERVINGS

3 tablespoons extra-virgin olive oil

2 tablespoons red wine vinegar or sherry vinegar

1 garlic clove, minced

¼ teaspoon fine sea salt

¼ teaspoon coarsely ground black pepper

Pinch of crushed red pepper flakes

3 to 4 heirloom tomatoes (about 1½ pounds), sliced or cut into wedges

8 ounces (about 2 balls) burrata cheese

Balsamic Glaze (page 22) or store-bought version

2 tablespoons chopped fresh basil or parsley

Crusty artisanal bread

This simply elegant summer dish highlights the vibrant flavors of heirloom tomatoes in all their colorful, juicy glory. A quick marinade of oil, vinegar, garlic, and herbs enhances their natural sweetness and acidity, while creamy burrata adds richness and contrast. Burrata is a fresh Italian cheese made from mozzarella and cream—the outer shell is solid mozzarella, while the inside is filled with soft curds and cream, lending a luscious texture to the meal.

1. Combine oil, vinegar, garlic, salt, black pepper, and red pepper flakes in a large bowl. Add tomatoes and toss gently to coat. Let mixture stand for 20 to 30 minutes.

2. Transfer marinated tomatoes to a serving platter, spooning any juices over top. Cut or tear burrata into large pieces and nestle them among tomatoes. Drizzle with Balsamic Glaze and sprinkle with basil. Serve at room temperature with bread.

TOMATO-AND-AVOCADO SALAD

MAKES 6 SERVINGS

¼ cup chopped fresh cilantro leaves
1 small garlic clove, minced
½ jalapeño, seeded and sliced
2 tablespoons brown sugar
2 teaspoons ground cumin
1 teaspoon ground coriander
¾ teaspoon fine sea salt
¼ teaspoon coarsely ground black pepper
1 teaspoon grated lime zest
⅓ cup fresh lime juice
2 tablespoons extra-virgin olive oil
1½ to 2 pounds heirloom tomatoes, cored and sliced
2 ripe avocados, sliced
Garnish: fresh cilantro leaves

This colorful salad pairs well with grilled meats, tacos, or any Southwestern-inspired meal. Juicy heirloom tomatoes bring sweetness and acidity, while creamy ripe avocados add richness, all tied together with a bold, zesty vinaigrette. To choose a perfectly ripe avocado, gently press near the stem—if it yields slightly without feeling mushy, it's ready to use.

1. Whisk together cilantro, garlic, jalapeño, brown sugar, cumin, coriander, salt, pepper, lime zest and juice, and oil in a small bowl. (Or combine in a jar, cover with lid, and shake until well blended.)
2. Arrange tomatoes and avocados on a platter. Drizzle with cilantro mixture and garnish, if desired.

WEDGE SALAD WITH BUTTERMILK–BLUE CHEESE DRESSING

MAKES 4 SERVINGS

This simple dish is a crisp, colorful take on a steakhouse classic. Feel free to swap in Gorgonzola for a slightly milder, earthy flavor.

1 large head iceberg lettuce, cored and cut into 4 wedges
2 tomatoes, thinly sliced or cut into wedges
1 carrot, julienned or grated
1 small cucumber, quartered and sliced
¼ cup cooked-and-crumbled bacon
Buttermilk-Blue Cheese Dressing (recipe at right)

Place wedges on individual salad plates. Top with tomatoes, carrots, and cucumber. Sprinkle with bacon and drizzle with Buttermilk-Blue Cheese Dressing. Serve with additional dressing.

BUTTERMILK–BLUE CHEESE DRESSING

½ cup buttermilk
⅓ cup mayonnaise
⅓ cup sour cream
1 tablespoon lemon juice
½ teaspoon fine sea salt
½ teaspoon coarsely ground black pepper
⅛ teaspoon garlic powder
2 ounces crumbled blue cheese or Gorgonzola

Combine buttermilk, mayonnaise, sour cream, juice, salt, pepper, and garlic powder in a blender. Blend until smooth. Add blue cheese; pulse until evenly blended. Dressing may be stirred together in a bowl for a chunkier texture. Makes about 1 cup.

CANTALOUPE-AND-BLUEBERRY SALAD WITH HONEY, LIME, AND MINT

MAKES 6 CUPS

This eye-catching salad pairs sweet cantaloupe and juicy blueberries with dragon fruit—an exotic fruit known for its vibrant pink skin and speckled white flesh. Dragon fruit has a mellow flavor similar to kiwi and pear. If you can't find dragon fruit, peeled and sliced kiwi makes an excellent substitute with a similar texture and tang. You can also substitute halved grapes, which are easily found in markets.

1 tablespoon honey
1 tablespoon lime juice
1 tablespoon chopped fresh mint
4 cups cantaloupe, cubed or balled
1 cup fresh blueberries
1 dragon fruit or kiwi, cubed or balled
Garnish: fresh mint sprigs or leaves

Whisk together honey, lime juice, and mint in a large bowl. Add cantaloupe, blueberries, and dragon fruit, tossing gently to coat. Garnish, if desired. Cover and chill until ready to serve.

CREAMY CUCUMBER-AND-SWEET ONION SALAD

MAKES 3½ CUPS

When summer gardens overflow with cucumbers, this creamy salad is a refreshing way to enjoy them. Crisp cucumber slices and mild, sweet onions are tossed in a tangy dressing that's simple yet full of flavor. This recipe makes just enough for a small batch, but it doubles easily for a crowd.

1 large seedless cucumber, thinly sliced
½ sweet onion, sliced
1 teaspoon kosher salt
¼ cup sour cream
1 tablespoon fresh or 1 teaspoon dried dill leaves
1½ teaspoons apple cider or white wine vinegar
½ teaspoon granulated sugar
Pinch of garlic powder
⅛ teaspoon coarsely ground black pepper

1. Combine cucumber and onion in a colander set over a pan or bowl. Sprinkle with salt, stirring until dispersed. Let stand for 30 minutes, stirring occasionally. Drain liquid, but do not rinse.

2. Combine sour cream, dill, vinegar, sugar, garlic powder, and pepper in a large bowl. Add cucumbers and onion, stirring until coated.

CELERY SALAD WITH DATES, WALNUTS, AND PARMESAN

MAKES 3 CUPS

Heavily inspired by New York Chef Nick Curtola of The Four Horsemen in Brooklyn, this tasty salad brings together all the best elements of a great dish—crunchy, soft, spicy, salty, and sweet. I often have extra celery and dates on hand, so I was thrilled to discover this recipe that puts both to delicious use.

- ⅓ cup extra-virgin olive oil
- 2 tablespoons lemon juice
- ½ teaspoon crushed red pepper flakes
- ½ teaspoons fine sea salt
- ½ cup fresh, soft pitted Medjool dates (about 8 or 9 large), chopped
- 8 celery ribs, thinly sliced
- ½ cup toasted walnuts and/or pistachios, roughly chopped
- 2 tablespoons chopped fresh mint leaves
- ⅓ cup (about 1½ ounces) coarsely grated fresh Parmesan cheese

1. Combine olive oil, lemon juice, red pepper flakes, and salt in a large bowl.
2. Stir in dates, celery, walnuts, mint, and cheese. Serve immediately or, for best results, cover and chill for 2 hours to allow flavors to blend.

MARINATED CELERY-AND-CHICKPEA SALAD WITH LEMON-SHALLOT VINAIGRETTE

MAKES ABOUT 4 CUPS

Letting the ingredients marinate enhances the flavors, making this a great make-ahead dish for lunches and picnics. Or try it as a light side to grilled meats or seafood.

1 (15-ounce) can chickpeas, rinsed and drained
4 celery ribs, thinly sliced
1 cup cherry tomatoes, halved
3 green onions, thinly sliced
¼ cup packed fresh parsley, chopped
2 tablespoons chopped fresh mint
Lemon-Shallot Vinaigrette (recipe at right)
½ cup crumbled feta cheese

Combine chickpeas, celery, tomatoes, green onions, parsley, and mint in a large bowl, tossing to coat. Add about ⅓ cup Lemon-Shallot Vinaigrette (or more to taste), tossing to coat. Sprinkle with feta, tossing gently. Serve with additional vinaigrette.

LEMON-SHALLOT VINAIGRETTE

⅓ cup extra-virgin olive oil
½ teaspoon grated lemon zest
¼ cup fresh lemon juice
1 teaspoon Dijon mustard
1½ teaspoons honey or maple syrup
½ shallot, minced
1 tablespoon chopped fresh oregano
¼ teaspoon crushed red pepper flakes
¼ teaspoon fine sea salt
⅛ teaspoon coarsely ground black pepper

Combine oil, lemon zest and juice, mustard, honey, shallot, oregano, red pepper flakes, salt, and black pepper in a jar. Cover tightly with lid and shake vigorously. Makes ⅔ cup.

CAULIFLOWER CHICKPEA SALAD BOWL WITH CURRY-TAHINI DRESSING

MAKES 6 CUPS

The dressing can be made ahead, allowing the flavors to develop even more over time.

½ head cauliflower, cut into very small florets
1 (15-ounce) can chickpeas, rinsed and drained
¼ cup extra-virgin olive oil
½ teaspoon ground cumin
¼ teaspoon smoked paprika
¼ teaspoon fine sea salt
¼ teaspoon coarsely ground black pepper
1 red bell pepper, chopped
¼ cup chopped fresh cilantro or parsley
¼ cup toasted slivered almonds
Curry-Tahini Dressing (recipe at right)

1. Combine cauliflower and chickpeas in a large bowl. Add oil, cumin, paprika, salt, and pepper, tossing to coat. Cover and let marinate for 3 to 8 hours in the refrigerator.
2. Stir bell pepper and cilantro into cauliflower mixture. Sprinkle with almonds. Drizzle with Curry-Tahini Dressing. Serve with additional dressing.

CURRY-TAHINI DRESSING

¼ cup tahini
2 tablespoons lemon juice
1 tablespoon olive oil
2 teaspoons honey or maple syrup
½ teaspoon curry powder
¼ teaspoon turmeric
1 small garlic clove, minced
¼ teaspoon fine sea salt
¼ teaspoon coarsely ground black pepper
2 to 3 tablespoons warm water (optional)

Whisk together tahini, juice, oil, honey, curry powder, turmeric, garlic, salt, and pepper in a bowl. Add 2 to 3 tablespoons water, if desired, to obtain a pourable consistency. Makes ⅔ cup.

HEARTS OF PALM, GRAPEFRUIT, AND AVOCADO SALAD

MAKES 3 CUPS

3 tablespoons extra-virgin olive oil

¼ teaspoon grated lime zest

2 tablespoons fresh lime juice

1 teaspoon honey

⅛ teaspoon fine sea salt

⅛ teaspoon coarsely ground black pepper

1 (14-ounce) can or ½ (25-ounce) jar hearts of palm, drained and sliced

1 red grapefruit, peeled and sectioned

1 avocado, diced

1 tablespoon minced red onion

Hearts of palm are the tender inner core of certain palm trees, prized for their delicate, slightly nutty flavor and crisp-yet-creamy texture. Often found canned or jarred, hearts of palm make a wonderful addition to salads, offering a refreshing contrast to creamy avocado and juicy grapefruit. As the ingredients are tender, stir them carefully so they don't fall apart.

Combine oil, lime zest and juice, honey, salt, and pepper in a bowl. Add hearts of palm, grapefruit, avocado, and onion, tossing very gently until coated. Serve as is or over greens.

COUSCOUS-TABBOULEH SALAD

MAKES ABOUT 4 CUPS

This bright, refreshing take on traditional tabbouleh swaps bulgur for couscous, making it a quick-and-effortless dish perfect for busy days. Fresh mint and lemon add bursts of flavor. Serve it chilled or at room temperature.

1 cup couscous
1 cup water
⅓ cup extra-virgin olive oil
½ teaspoon grated lemon zest
¼ cup fresh lemon juice
1 teaspoon fine sea salt
¼ teaspoon coarsely ground black pepper
2 cups packed fresh flat-leaf parsley, chopped
1 (0.5-ounce) package fresh mint (about ½ cup lightly packed), chopped
1 cup cherry tomatoes, halved
½ seedless cucumber, quartered and sliced
2 green onions, sliced

1. Combine couscous and 1 cup water in a bowl; soak for 20 minutes or until couscous is tender. Stir with a fork to fluff.
2. Combine oil, lemon zest and juice, salt, and pepper in a bowl. Drizzle over couscous mixture, tossing to coat.
3. Stir in parsley, mint, cherry tomatoes, cucumber, and green onions.

MEDITERRANEAN WHITE BEAN SALAD

MAKES 4 SIDE-DISH SERVINGS

⅓ cup extra-virgin olive oil

¼ cup red or white wine vinegar

½ teaspoon whole-grain Dijon mustard

¼ teaspoon fine sea salt

¼ teaspoon coarsely ground black pepper

1 garlic clove, minced

1 (15-ounce) can cannellini, garbanzo, or another white bean, rinsed and drained

1 pint or 2 cups cherry tomatoes, halved

1 zucchini, yellow squash, or cucumber, cubed

2 tablespoons chopped fresh basil

Garnish: fresh basil sprigs

Once the garden gets going, I seem to have an endless supply of cherry tomatoes, squash, and fragrant basil. This quick side dish is a simple way to make the most of that fresh summer bounty. A can of white beans adds protein and heartiness, turning this bright, herb-filled mixture into a satisfying light meal or a flavorful side dish. Tossed with a simple dressing, this salad is easy to throw together and gets even better as it sits, making it perfect for picnics, potlucks, or a quick summer lunch.

1. Combine olive oil, vinegar, mustard, salt, pepper, and garlic in a medium-size bowl.

2. Stir in beans, tomatoes, and zucchini. Sprinkle with basil. Garnish, if desired.

Tomato, White Bean, and Tuna Salad: Follow recipe above and add 1 (5-ounce) can tuna, drained. Makes 4 servings.

HEIRLOOM TOMATO PANZANELLA WITH BRIE AND BASIL

MAKES 4 SERVINGS

8 ounces crusty artisan bread such as rosemary sourdough

3 to 4 large heirloom tomatoes (about 1½ pounds), cut into wedges or chunks

1 seedless cucumber, sliced or chopped

8 ounces Brie or fresh mozzarella, cubed

½ cup pitted Kalamata olives, halved

¼ small red onion, cut into slivers

⅓ cup extra-virgin olive oil

3 tablespoons sherry or red wine vinegar

1 small garlic clove, minced

¼ teaspoon fine sea salt

¼ teaspoon coarsely ground black pepper

⅓ cup fresh basil leaves, torn or thinly sliced

Serve a pretty bowlful of summer elegance when you place this on the table. Panzanella, a traditional Italian dish of bread and tomatoes, tastes every bit as beautiful as it looks.

This colorful take on a classic dish celebrates summer's best produce with juicy heirloom tomatoes, crisp cucumber, briny Kalamata olives, and fragrant basil. Cubes of crusty artisan bread soak up a simple-yet-bold dressing made from mild extra-virgin olive oil and sherry vinegar. Instead of the usual Parmesan, this version features creamy cubes of Brie or fresh mozzarella for a luxurious touch. It's rustic, refreshing, and ideal as a light meal or side for grilled fare.

1. Toast bread until dry and a light golden brown. Tear or cut into bite-size pieces. Let cool.

2. Combine tomatoes, cucumber, cheese, olives, and onion in a large bowl. Add toasted bread cubes, tossing to combine.

3. Whisk together olive oil, vinegar, and garlic in a small bowl; add salt and pepper. Pour over salad and toss gently to coat.

4. Let stand at room temperature for 20 to 30 minutes, tossing occasionally, so bread can absorb liquids.

5. Sprinkle with basil and toss mixture gently just before serving at room temperature.

MOROCCAN KALE-AND-GRAIN SALAD WITH CUMIN-CORIANDER VINAIGRETTE

MAKES 8 CUPS

Serve this as a light lunch, a side dish, or a base for grilled meats or roasted vegetables.

- 8 cups chopped fresh kale (about 10 ounces)
- 1 tablespoon extra-virgin olive oil
- ¼ teaspoon fine sea salt
- 3 cups cooked quinoa, bulgur, farro, or couscous
- ⅓ cup golden raisins or chopped dried apricots
- ⅓ cup toasted almonds or pistachios, chopped
- 2 green onions, thinly sliced
- Cumin-Coriander Vinaigrette (recipe at right)
- Garnish: lemon slices

1. Combine kale, oil, and salt in a large zip-top plastic bag. Massage for 1 minute or until kale is tender and darkened. Transfer kale mixture to a large bowl.
2. Stir in quinoa, raisins, almonds, and green onions. Drizzle with ⅓ cup Cumin-Coriander Vinaigrette, tossing to coat. Garnish, if desired. Serve with additional dressing.

CUMIN-CORIANDER VINAIGRETTE

- 1½ teaspoons ground coriander
- 1 teaspoon ground cumin
- ½ teaspoon fine sea salt
- ½ teaspoon coarsely ground black pepper
- ¼ teaspoon ground cinnamon
- ½ cup extra-virgin olive oil
- 2 tablespoons fresh lemon juice
- 2 teaspoons honey or maple syrup

Combine coriander, cumin, salt, pepper, cinnamon, oil, lemon juice, and honey in a jar. Cover with lid and shake vigorously until well blended. Cover and refrigerate until ready to use. Shake before serving. Makes ¾ cup.

STRAWBERRY-SPINACH SALAD WITH TOASTED PECANS AND HONEY-POPPY SEED DRESSING

MAKES 4 SERVINGS

Nothing says spring like a spinach salad with vibrant strawberries. The combination of juicy strawberries, crisp baby spinach, and crunchy toasted pecans is simple yet elegant. A creamy poppy seed dressing ties everything together with just the right balance of tang and sweetness.

9 ounces baby spinach

1 (16-ounce) container fresh strawberries, sliced

½ cup toasted or candied pecans or hazelnuts, roughly chopped

¼ cup thinly sliced red onion

Honey-Poppy Seed Dressing (recipe at right)

⅓ cup crumbled blue, feta, or goat cheese

Place spinach, strawberries, pecans, and onion in a large bowl, and add just enough Honey-Poppy Seed Dressing (about ⅓ cup) to lightly coat greens. Toss gently to coat. Keep in bowl or divide among 4 individual salad bowls. Sprinkle with cheese. Serve with additional dressing.

HONEY-POPPY SEED DRESSING

¼ cup apple cider vinegar

¼ cup extra-virgin olive oil

¼ cup honey

1 tablespoon poppy seeds

1 teaspoon grated white onion (optional)

½ teaspoon dry mustard

½ teaspoon fine sea salt

⅛ teaspoon coarsely ground black pepper

Combine vinegar; oil; honey; poppy seeds; onion, if desired; mustard; salt; and pepper in a jar. Cover and shake vigorously. Store in the refrigerator for up to 5 days. Shake before serving. Makes ¾ cup.

CHOPPED SALAD WITH AVOCADO-RANCH DRESSING

MAKES 4 SERVINGS

Avocado makes a dressing extra rich and delicious. If you don't have buttermilk, use regular milk and add an extra tablespoon of lemon juice to approximate buttermilk's unique flavor. Use any leftover dressing for a yummy vegetable dip.

- 2 heads romaine lettuce, coarsely chopped (8 cups lightly packed)
- 2 tomatoes, cut into wedges
- 1 cucumber, quartered and sliced
- 2 avocados, sliced
- Avocado-Ranch Dressing (recipe at right)
- 4 to 6 slices cooked bacon, coarsely chopped
- Coarsely ground black pepper

Arrange lettuce, tomatoes, cucumber, and avocado slices on a large platter or on individual salad plates. Drizzle with Avocado-Ranch Dressing and sprinkle evenly with bacon and pepper. Serve with additional dressing.

AVOCADO-RANCH DRESSING

- 1 avocado, chopped
- ¼ cup mayonnaise
- ¼ cup sour cream
- ½ cup buttermilk
- 2 tablespoons lemon juice
- 1 tablespoon chopped fresh basil
- 1 tablespoon chopped fresh or 1 teaspoon dried dill
- ¼ teaspoon fine sea salt
- 2 to 3 tablespoons water (optional)

Combine avocado, mayonnaise, sour cream, buttermilk, juice, basil, dill, and salt in a blender. Process until smooth. Add 2 to 3 tablespoons water, if desired, to obtain a pourable consistency. Cover and chill until ready to serve. Store leftovers in the refrigerator for up to 3 days. Makes 1⅔ cups.

SIMPLE SIDE SALAD WITH BLENDED GINGER DRESSING

MAKES 6 SERVINGS

This dish is just like the flavorful salad that's served at Japanese steakhouses—bright, bold, and incredibly refreshing.

6 cups shredded or sliced iceberg or romaine lettuce
2 cups shredded purple cabbage
2 carrots, grated
Blended Ginger Dressing (recipe at right)

Combine lettuce, cabbage, and carrots in a large bowl. Divide evenly among salad bowls or plates and drizzle with Blended Ginger Dressing. Serve with additional dressing.

BLENDED GINGER DRESSING

This tangy recipe is made by blending onion, celery, fresh ginger, and a few pantry staples into a smooth, pourable dressing with just a hint of texture. The result is a zippy, slightly sweet vinaigrette that pairs perfectly with crisp iceberg or mixed greens. Quick to make and easy to keep on hand, it adds big flavor to simple salads.

½ cup minced onion
½ cup avocado, peanut, or mild-flavored olive oil
⅓ cup rice wine vinegar
2 tablespoons water
2 tablespoons minced fresh ginger
2 tablespoons minced celery
2 tablespoons ketchup
1½ tablespoons soy sauce
2 teaspoons lemon juice
1 small garlic clove, minced
¼ to ½ teaspoon fine sea salt
¼ teaspoon coarsely ground black pepper

Combine onion, oil, vinegar, 2 tablespoons water, ginger, celery, ketchup, soy sauce, lemon juice, garlic, salt, and pepper in a blender. Blend until smooth. Makes 1 cup.

KALE SALAD WITH ORANGE-SESAME DRESSING

MAKES 6 SERVINGS

This colorful kale salad is simply packed with color, crunch, and flavor. Shredded purple cabbage, bright carrots, and green onions bring freshness, while dried cranberries add a touch of sweetness. The dressing ties it all together with a perfect balance of citrus and umami. Kale can be tough when raw, but a quick massage with a little dressing transforms it into a tender green.

1 (16-ounce) package chopped kale
Orange-Sesame Dressing (recipe at right)
2 cups shredded purple cabbage
1 cup shredded or julienned carrots
3 green onions, thinly sliced
½ cup dried cranberries
½ cup chopped toasted cashews

1. Place kale in a large bowl and drizzle ¼ cup Orange-Sesame Dressing over top. Massage with hands for 2 minutes or until kale leaves soften.
2. Add cabbage, carrots, onions, and cranberries to bowl, tossing to coat. Drizzle with additional dressing until salad is coated. Sprinkle with nuts.

ORANGE-SESAME DRESSING

1 teaspoon grated orange zest
½ cup fresh orange juice
3 tablespoons rice vinegar
1 tablespoon soy sauce or tamari
1 tablespoon extra-virgin olive oil
2 teaspoons toasted sesame oil
1 tablespoon honey
1 small garlic clove, minced
½ teaspoon fine sea salt

Combine orange zest and juice, vinegar, soy sauce, olive oil, sesame oil, honey, garlic, and salt in a jar; cover lid tightly and shake vigorously. Makes ¾ cup.

BIBB SALAD WITH RASPBERRIES, MANGO, HAZELNUTS, GOAT CHEESE, AND RASPBERRY VINAIGRETTE

MAKES 4 SERVINGS

This salad is a delightful mix of tender Bibb lettuce, sweet raspberries and mango slices, crunchy toasted hazelnuts, and creamy goat cheese (ricotta makes a fine substitution). A quick homemade Raspberry Vinaigrette ties everything together with a balance of tangy and fruity flavors.

2 heads Bibb lettuce, torn into bite-size pieces
1 mango, peeled and sliced into thin strips
¾ cup fresh or frozen-and-thawed raspberries
⅓ cup crumbled goat cheese or ricotta
⅓ cup toasted hazelnuts, roughly chopped
Raspberry Vinaigrette (recipe at right)

Arrange lettuce on a platter or individual plates. Top evenly with mango slices and raspberries. Sprinkle evenly with goat cheese and hazelnuts. Drizzle with Raspberry Vinaigrette just before serving. Serve with additional vinaigrette.

RASPBERRY VINAIGRETTE

1 cup fresh or frozen-and-thawed raspberries
¼ cup white balsamic vinegar
1 tablespoon granulated sugar
¼ cup extra-virgin olive oil
¼ teaspoon fine sea salt
¼ teaspoon coarsely ground black pepper

Place raspberries in a fine wire-mesh strainer placed over a bowl; mash until smooth. Discard seeds. Whisk in vinegar, sugar, oil, salt, and pepper. You can also combine all ingredients in a blender. Blend until well combined. Pour, in batches, through a fine wire-mesh strainer placed over a bowl. Makes about 1 cup.

BEET, ORANGE, AND BLUE CHEESE SALAD WITH TARRAGON VINAIGRETTE

MAKES 4 SERVINGS

This boldly flavored salad brings together a striking combination of color and flavor.

4 cups mixed baby salad greens

1 (8-ounce) package refrigerated cooked beets, diced

2 seedless oranges, peeled and sectioned

½ cup crumbled or diced Roquefort or blue cheese

½ cup toasted walnuts or hazelnuts

Tarragon Vinaigrette (recipe at right)

Place greens in a large serving bowl or in individual salad bowls. Top evenly with beets, orange segments, and cheese. Sprinkle with nuts. Drizzle with Tarragon Vinaigrette. Serve with additional vinaigrette.

TARRAGON VINAIGRETTE

½ cup extra-virgin olive oil

3 tablespoons sherry vinegar

2 tablespoons white wine vinegar

1 teaspoon whole-grain or Dijon mustard

1 teaspoon honey

1 tablespoon finely chopped fresh tarragon

½ teaspoon fine sea salt

½ teaspoon coarsely ground black pepper

Combine oil, vinegars, mustard, honey, tarragon, salt, and pepper in a jar; cover and shake vigorously. For a finer texture, place ingredients in a small food processor and process until well blended. Makes ¾ cup.

SIMPLE BEET-AND-ARUGULA SALAD WITH WHIPPED RICOTTA AND HONEY VINAIGRETTE

MAKES 4 SERVINGS

This salad layers bold flavors and contrasting textures for a dish that feels restaurant-worthy yet is simple to prepare. Roasted or steamed beets pair beautifully with peppery arugula and crunchy toasted nuts, all set over a creamy bed of whipped ricotta sweetened with a touch of honey. A lovely vinaigrette balances the richness of the ricotta and brings it all together.

1 (15-ounce) container whole-milk ricotta cheese

2 tablespoons extra-virgin olive oil

1 tablespoon honey

¼ teaspoon fine sea salt

4 to 6 cups baby arugula

Honey Vinaigrette (recipe at right)

1 (8-ounce) package cooked beets

⅓ cup toasted walnuts or pistachios, coarsely chopped

1. Combine ricotta, oil, honey, and salt in a food processor. Process until smooth and creamy. Spread evenly on bottom of a serving platter or individual plates.

2. Place arugula in a large bowl. Pour about ¼ cup Honey Vinaigrette over greens and toss gently to coat. Arrange evenly over ricotta mixture.

3. Slice or quarter beets and place in a mixing bowl. Add about 1 tablespoon vinaigrette and stir until beets are coated. Arrange beets evenly over greens. Sprinkle evenly with nuts. Serve with additional vinaigrette.

HONEY VINAIGRETTE

½ shallot, minced

¼ cup white balsamic vinegar or apple cider vinegar

2 tablespoons honey

½ teaspoon fine sea salt

¼ teaspoon coarsely ground black pepper

½ cup extra-virgin olive oil

Combine shallot, vinegar, honey, salt, pepper, and oil in a jar. Cover and shake vigorously until well blended. Shake again before serving. Makes about ¾ cup.

CARROT, MANGO, AND JICAMA SLAW

MAKES 6 CUPS

½ teaspoon lime zest
¼ cup fresh lime juice
1 tablespoon granulated sugar
1 tablespoon extra-virgin olive oil
1 teaspoon ground cumin
1 teaspoon fine sea salt
¼ teaspoon coarsely ground black pepper
4 large carrots, julienned
2 firm-but-ripe mangoes, julienned
1 small jicama (about 1 pound), peeled and julienned
¼ cup chopped fresh cilantro
½ to 1 jalapeño pepper, seeded and sliced

This refreshing side dish is all about texture and flavor. Vegetables and fruit are julienned using a mandolin or handheld peeler, creating thin strips that soak up the delicious dressing while staying crisp. Choose a firm mango for best results—if it's too ripe, the flesh will be too soft to shred and is better diced. This slaw makes a colorful side for tacos, grilled meats, or sandwiches and holds up well for potlucks and picnics.

1. Stir together lime zest and juice, sugar, oil, cumin, salt, and pepper in a large bowl. Stir in carrots, mangoes, jicama, cilantro, and jalapeño.

2. Cover and refrigerate until ready to serve. Stir just before serving.

TEX-MEX COLESLAW WITH CREAMY LIME-CHIPOTLE DRESSING

MAKES 10 CUPS

8 cups shredded cabbage (green, red, or a mix)

1 (15.5-ounce) can black beans, rinsed and drained

1 cup corn kernels (fresh, frozen, or canned and drained)

1 red, yellow, or orange bell pepper, diced

⅓ cup chopped fresh cilantro (optional)

½ cup mayonnaise

⅓ cup sour cream

½ teaspoon lime zest

2 tablespoons fresh lime juice

1 tablespoon Mexican seasoning blend or 1½ teaspoons ground cumin plus 1½ teaspoons ground chili powder

1 teaspoon fine sea salt

¼ teaspoon coarsely ground black pepper

1 to 2 teaspoons finely chopped chipotle peppers in adobo sauce (optional)

This zesty slaw is a colorful, crunchy side dish that makes an ideal contribution to cook-outs, potlucks, or taco night. Shredded cabbage forms the crisp base, while black beans, corn, and chopped bell pepper add texture and heartiness. The creamy dressing brings it all together. For a smoky, spicy kick, stir in some finely chopped chipotle peppers in adobo sauce.

1. Combine cabbage, black beans, corn, bell pepper, and cilantro, if desired, in a large bowl.

2. To make dressing, whisk together mayonnaise; sour cream; lime zest and juice; Mexican seasoning blend; salt; pepper; and, if desired, chipotle peppers until smooth. Pour over cabbage mixture and toss until evenly coated.

3. Cover and refrigerate for at least 30 minutes before serving to let flavors blend. Stir again just before serving.

RAMEN NOODLE SLAW

MAKES ABOUT 12 CUPS

- 2 (6-ounce) packages soy, beef, or other flavor ramen noodles
- ½ cup avocado, vegetable, or mild-flavored olive oil
- ⅓ cup granulated sugar
- ¼ cup apple cider vinegar
- 2 (14-ounce) packages shredded coleslaw mix
- ½ cup roasted sunflower seeds
- 1 (5-ounce) package sweetened dried cranberries
- 4 green onions, chopped

> When you need to bring a large side dish to a gathering, this slaw is a well-loved solution. The sweetness and crunch combine in an appealing complement to any potluck. Best of all, you only have to chop one ingredient!

When we lived in Birmingham, Alabama, we shared many cherished meals and memories around the dinner table with our wonderful neighbor Colleen Burroughs. One dish she still brings to gatherings is a sweet, tangy slaw with just the right crunch—always a crowd favorite. As Colleen says, "I make this size for a crowd or a potluck. It can easily be cut in half for a smaller table. I keep the ingredients in the pantry ready for a crowd and just grab the slaw and green onions. I also like leftovers the next day when it has been marinating in the fridge. I have literally put this together in the back hatch of an SUV for a church party. It never disappoints."

1. Without opening noodle packages, crush noodles into small pieces with hands or a rolling pin. Open packages and carefully remove seasoning packets.
2. To make dressing, whisk together oil, sugar, vinegar, and contents of seasoning packets in a very large bowl. (Dressing may be made ahead and stored, covered, in the refrigerator for up to 1 day.)
3. Stir in coleslaw mix, crushed noodles, sunflower seeds, dried cranberries, and green onions, tossing until well coated. Cover and chill until ready to serve.

Variation: Substitute 1 (12-ounce) bag broccoli slaw for one of the bags of coleslaw mix. If using a whole cabbage, shred about 12 to 14 cups and add 2 shredded carrots to the mix. One (14-ounce) bag of coleslaw mix yields about 6½ cups.

MAIN-DISH SALADS and BOWLS

- 116 Lemony Herbed Chicken Salad
- 117 Quick Curried Chicken Salad
- 118 Chicken Waldorf Salad
- 119 Southern Chicken, Tomato, and Black-eyed Pea Salad
- 120 Easy Chicken Cobb Salad with Dijon Vinaigrette
- 122 Mexican Chicken Cobb Salad with Chipotle Ranch Dressing
- 123 Chicken Caesar Salad with Chipotle Dressing
- 124 Crispy Fried Chicken Salad with Honey-Mustard Dressing
- 125 Chicken-and-Napa Cabbage Salad with Sesame-Soy Vinaigrette
- 126 Chicken, Orange, and Hazelnut Salad Bowl with Honey-Orange Dressing
- 127 Chicken-and-Grain Bowl with Creamy Green Goddess Dressing
- 128 Spicy Chicken-and-Mango Salad Bowl with Cilantro-Lime Vinaigrette
- 129 Chicken Noodle Bowl with Peanut-Coconut Dressing
- 130 Chicken Salad Bowl with Five-Spice Vinaigrette
- 131 Chicken Burrito Bowl with Creamy Chipotle Dressing
- 132 Greek Chicken Rice Bowl with Tzatziki Dressing
- 134 Za'atar Chicken, Bulgur, and Lentil Salad Bowl
- 135 Salad Bowl with Curried Miso Dressing
- 136 Steak, Corn, and Tomato Salad with Smoky Cumin Vinaigrette
- 137 Beefsteak Salad with Blue Cheese-Balsamic Vinaigrette
- 138 Roast Beef Salad with Heirloom Tomatoes and Thai Dressing
- 139 Watercress-and-Roast Beef Salad with Chimichurri Vinaigrette
- 140 Hearty Cuban Salad with Mojo Vinaigrette
- 141 Antipasto Salad with Marinated Artichokes, Beans, Slivered Meats, and Creamy Hummus Dressing
- 142 Tuna Niçoise Salad with Caper-Shallot Vinaigrette
- 143 Fall Greens with Smoked Trout, Pear, Cranberry, and Date Vinaigrette
- 144 Smoked Sockeye Caesar Salad with Lemony Dressing
- 145 Quinoa-and-Smoked Salmon Kale Bowl with Lemon-Tahini Dressing
- 146 Smoked Salmon-and-Beet Salad with Gribiche Dressing
- 147 California Roll Bowl
- 148 Shrimp-and-Glass Noodle Salad
- 149 Shrimp-and-Hoppin' John Salad
- 150 Crawfish Rémoulade

LEMONY HERBED CHICKEN SALAD

MAKES 5 CUPS

½ cup mayonnaise

¼ cup sour cream

1 teaspoon Dijon mustard

½ teaspoon lemon zest

2 tablespoons fresh lemon juice

½ teaspoon fine sea salt

¼ teaspoon coarsely ground black pepper

¼ cup lightly packed fresh basil, chopped

2 tablespoons chopped fresh tarragon

1 tablespoon chopped fresh chives

4 cups shredded or chopped rotisserie or cooked chicken

1 cup finely chopped celery

Garnishes: lemon slices, fresh rosemary sprig

Nothing brightens up a classic chicken salad like a generous mix of fresh herbs. This version combines tender rotisserie or cooked chicken with fragrant basil, delicate tarragon, and mild chives, creating a refreshing and aromatic dish. For an interesting variation, add ½ cup halved red seedless grapes.

1 Combine mayonnaise, sour cream, mustard, lemon zest and juice, salt, and pepper in a large bowl. Stir in basil, tarragon, and chives.

2 Add chicken and celery, stirring until well blended. Garnish, if desired.

QUICK CURRIED CHICKEN SALAD

MAKES 4½ CUPS

½ cup mayonnaise
⅓ cup mango chutney
¼ cup sour cream
1½ tablespoons curry powder
3 cups cooked, shredded chicken
¼ cup toasted sliced almonds
¼ cup dried cranberries
5 green onions, thinly sliced

Sweet, savory, and spiced just right, this curried chicken salad is exciting to eat. The warm flavors of curry powder pair beautifully with tender chicken, while mango chutney adds a touch of sweetness and depth. Dried cranberries provide a tart contrast, balancing the dish with a bit of chewiness. Whether served on a bed of greens, tucked into a sandwich, or spooned into lettuce cups, this salad is a simple-yet-flavorful option for lunch or a light dinner.

Combine mayonnaise, chutney, sour cream, and curry powder in a large bowl. Stir in chicken, almonds, cranberries, and green onions. Cover and chill until ready to serve.

CHICKEN WALDORF SALAD

MAKES 8 CUPS

This better-than-basic chicken salad offers a fresh take on a favorite. Tender cooked chicken meets crisp apples, grapes, celery, and toasted walnuts—all tossed in a creamy dressing that ties everything together and helps keep the apples from browning. It's hearty, refreshing, and travels well—just what you need for your next gathering. Leftover grilled chicken makes a delicious substitute.

- ½ cup mayonnaise
- ¼ cup sour cream
- 2 teaspoons lemon juice
- 1 tablespoon honey
- ¼ teaspoon fine sea salt
- ¼ teaspoon coarsely ground black pepper
- 2 cups shredded cooked chicken
- 3 celery ribs, finely chopped
- ⅓ cup chopped toasted walnuts
- 2 red or green apples, cored and chopped
- ½ cup red or green seedless grapes, halved

1. Stir together mayonnaise, sour cream, lemon juice, honey, salt, and pepper in a large bowl.
2. Stir in shredded chicken. Add chopped celery, walnuts, apples, and grapes, stirring until evenly combined. Cover and refrigerate until ready to serve.

SOUTHERN CHICKEN, TOMATO, AND BLACK-EYED PEA SALAD

MAKES 4 SERVINGS

½ cup extra-virgin olive oil
½ teaspoon lemon zest
3 tablespoons fresh lemon juice
2 tablespoons chopped fresh basil
2 small garlic cloves, minced
½ to 1 jalapeño pepper, seeded and minced
¼ teaspoon fine sea salt
¼ teaspoon coarsely ground black pepper
2 (15.5-ounce) cans black-eyed peas, rinsed and drained
4 cups loose-leaf salad greens
4 slices bacon, cooked and crumbled
3 large heirloom tomatoes, sliced
8 to 12 small fried chicken tenders, sliced

I'm not fond of heating up the kitchen by cooking dried peas on a hot day, so I go for canned. Adding cooked crumbled bacon and sliced strips of fried chicken tenders makes it a filling entrée salad. Bring home takeout strips, use leftovers, or substitute some shredded rotisserie chicken.

1. Whisk together oil, lemon zest and juice, basil, garlic, jalapeño, salt, and pepper in a large bowl.
2. Stir in black-eyed peas, tossing gently. Cover and chill for several hours, if desired, to allow flavors to marry.
3. Divide greens evenly into 4 large salad bowls. Top evenly with black-eyed pea mixture, reserving liquid. Top evenly with bacon, sliced tomatoes, and chicken. Use liquid from black-eyed pea mixture as a dressing.

EASY CHICKEN COBB SALAD WITH DIJON VINAIGRETTE

MAKES 4 SERVINGS

This no-cook salad is packed with bold flavors and fresh ingredients, making it a perfect meal for busy days. Using precooked grilled chicken, crispy bacon, and hard-boiled eggs, it comes together effortlessly.

6 cups chopped romaine, iceberg, or other lettuce

2 cups precooked grilled chicken strips or 4 small cooked chicken breasts, sliced

4 hard-boiled eggs, peeled and chopped

2 tomatoes, seeded and chopped

2 avocados, diced

1 seedless cucumber, sliced

6 to 8 slices bacon, cooked and crumbled

¼ red onion, thinly sliced

½ cup crumbled blue cheese

Dijon Vinaigrette (recipe at right)

Coarsely ground black pepper (optional)

Divide lettuce evenly into 4 large shallow bowls. Arrange chicken, eggs, tomatoes, avocados, cucumber, bacon, onion, and blue cheese on top of greens. Drizzle with Dijon Vinaigrette. Sprinkle with pepper, if desired.

DIJON VINAIGRETTE

This vinaigrette can be made with fresh or dried herbs and fresh or dried garlic powder. Fresh herbs tend to wilt and darken, so use any remaining dressing within a day for best flavor. If using dried oregano and garlic powder, you can store leftovers in the refrigerator for up to a week. The leftover dressing makes a great marinade for chicken breasts.

⅓ cup extra-virgin olive oil

3 tablespoons red wine vinegar

1 tablespoon lemon juice

1 tablespoon water

1½ teaspoons dried oregano or 1 tablespoon fresh chopped oregano

1½ teaspoons Dijon mustard

½ teaspoon garlic powder or 1 small minced fresh garlic clove

½ teaspoon honey

¼ teaspoon fine sea salt

¼ teaspoon coarsely ground black pepper

Combine oil, vinegar, lemon juice, 1 tablespoon water, oregano, mustard, garlic powder, honey, salt, and pepper in a jar. Cover with lid and shake vigorously. Makes ⅔ cup.

MEXICAN CHICKEN COBB SALAD WITH CHIPOTLE RANCH DRESSING

MAKES 4 SERVINGS

Mexican-inspired Cobb salad swaps out traditional ingredients for bold Southwest flavors. Instead of bacon and blue cheese, this version features black beans, corn, and creamy avocado. Precooked chicken makes it quick to assemble, while a smoky dressing ties everything together.

6 cups chopped romaine lettuce
¼ cup chopped fresh cilantro
3 cups cooked chicken, cubed or chopped
1 cup canned black beans, rinsed and drained
1 cup corn kernels (fresh, frozen, or canned)
1 cup cherry tomatoes, halved
1 avocado, diced
½ cup shredded cheddar or cotija cheese
4 thin slices red onion
2 hard-boiled eggs, sliced or chopped
Tortilla strips or crushed tortilla chips
Chipotle Ranch Dressing (recipe at right)

1. Arrange greens and cilantro on a large serving platter or on individual plates. Top evenly with chicken, beans, corn, tomatoes, avocado, cheese, onion, and eggs.
2. Top with tortilla strips and drizzle with Chipotle Ranch Dressing. Serve with additional dressing.

CHIPOTLE RANCH DRESSING

¼ cup mayonnaise
¼ cup sour cream
1 tablespoon milk
1 tablespoon lime juice
½ teaspoon white vinegar
½ teaspoon garlic powder
½ teaspoon onion powder
¼ teaspoon smoked paprika (optional)
½ to 1 teaspoon chipotle peppers in adobo sauce, finely minced
2 teaspoons chopped fresh cilantro
¼ teaspoon fine sea salt
⅛ teaspoon coarsely ground black pepper
1 to 2 tablespoons water

Whisk together mayonnaise; sour cream; milk; lime juice; vinegar; garlic powder; onion powder; paprika, if desired; chipotle peppers; cilantro; salt; and pepper. Stir in 1 to 2 tablespoons water to obtain a pourable consistency. Make ¾ cup.

CHICKEN CAESAR SALAD WITH CHIPOTLE DRESSING

MAKES 4 SERVINGS

This high-flavor salad puts a smoky, spicy spin on the original version. To complement the flavors, store-bought croutons are given an easy upgrade—tossed with chili powder, paprika, and cumin after a quick mist of cooking spray for extra crunch and flavor.

3 heads romaine lettuce, torn
1 red bell pepper, thinly sliced
1 yellow bell pepper, thinly sliced
Chipotle Dressing (recipe at right)
3 cups shredded cooked chicken or grilled chicken, cut into strips
⅓ cup shredded Parmesan cheese
Chili Croutons (recipe below)

Combine lettuce and bell peppers in a large bowl. Add about ⅓ cup Chipotle Dressing, tossing to coat. Divide salad evenly onto 4 serving plates. Arrange chicken evenly over salad. Sprinkle evenly with Parmesan and Chili Croutons. Serve with additional dressing.

Chili Croutons: Spray **2 cups store-bought croutons** lightly with vegetable cooking spray; place in a plastic bag or bowl. Combine **1 teaspoon paprika, ½ teaspoon ground chili powder,** and **½ teaspoon ground cumin** in a small bowl. Add to croutons; shake vigorously or stir to coat. Makes 2 cups.

CHIPOTLE DRESSING

The creamy dressing gets a lively kick from chipotle peppers in adobo sauce, adding depth and just the right amount of heat. To avoid the raw eggs usually used in Caesar dressings, this one is blended with hard-boiled eggs.

¼ cup extra-virgin olive oil
2 hard-boiled eggs
2 tablespoons cider vinegar
1 tablespoon lemon juice
2 teaspoons chipotle peppers in adobo sauce
1 teaspoon Worcestershire sauce
½ teaspoon anchovy paste
1 clove garlic, minced
¼ teaspoon fine sea salt

Combine oil, eggs, cider vinegar, lemon juice, chipotle peppers, Worcestershire sauce, anchovy paste, garlic, and salt in a blender. Process until well blended. Makes ¾ cup.

CRISPY FRIED CHICKEN SALAD WITH HONEY-MUSTARD DRESSING

MAKES 4 SERVINGS

This fried chicken salad is a perfect balance of crisp chicken tenders; fresh vegetables; and a creamy, sweet-tangy dressing. Using store-bought fried chicken tenders makes for an easy lunch or dinner. Serve it with warm cornbread or garlic toast for a Southern-inspired feast!

6 cups mixed salad greens (romaine, spinach, or iceberg)

1 cup cherry tomatoes, halved

1 seedless cucumber, quartered and sliced

1 carrot, julienned or grated

¼ to ½ cup (1 to 2 ounces) shredded cheddar or Colby-Jack cheese

¼ cup thinly sliced red onion or Vidalia onion

8 to 12 fried chicken tenders, sliced

¼ cup chopped crispy bacon (optional)

¼ cup toasted pecans or sunflower seeds (optional)

Honey-Mustard Dressing (recipe at right)

Arrange greens on a large platter or on individual salad plates. Top evenly with tomatoes, cucumber, carrot, cheese, and onion. Top evenly with chicken and sprinkle with bacon and nuts, if desired. Drizzle with Honey-Mustard Dressing. Serve with additional dressing.

HONEY-MUSTARD DRESSING

¼ cup Dijon or coarse-ground mustard

¼ cup honey

2 tablespoons apple cider vinegar

2 tablespoons mayonnaise

¼ teaspoon fine sea salt

Combine mustard, honey, vinegar, mayonnaise, and salt in a jar. Cover with lid and shake vigorously. Makes ¾ cup.

CHICKEN-AND-NAPA CABBAGE SALAD WITH SESAME-SOY VINAIGRETTE

MAKES 4 SERVINGS

This light, refreshing dish comes together effortlessly, making it a great solution for an easy weeknight meal. The combination of textures—crunchy cabbage, juicy chicken, and crisp bell pepper—makes each bite satisfying, while the sesame seeds add a subtle nuttiness.

6 cups thinly sliced Napa cabbage (about 1 head)

2 cups shredded red cabbage

1 yellow bell pepper, thinly sliced

1 cup snow peas, trimmed

4 cooked boneless, skinless chicken breasts, sliced

1 teaspoon sesame seeds

Sesame-Soy Vinaigrette (recipe at right)

Combine cabbages, bell pepper, and snow peas in a large bowl. Add chicken, tossing well. Sprinkle with sesame seeds. Pour Sesame-Soy Vinaigrette over cabbage mixture, stirring to coat.

SESAME-SOY VINAIGRETTE

2 tablespoons soy sauce

2 tablespoons rice wine vinegar

2 tablespoons sesame oil

¼ cup extra-virgin olive oil

1 teaspoon grated fresh ginger

½ teaspoon granulated sugar

Combine soy sauce, vinegar, sesame oil, olive oil, ginger, and sugar in a jar; tighten lid and shake vigorously. Makes ⅔ cup.

CHICKEN, ORANGE, AND HAZELNUT SALAD BOWL WITH HONEY-ORANGE DRESSING

MAKES 4 SERVINGS

This salad is a delicious mix of fresh, bright flavors and satisfying textures. Tender rotisserie chicken, juicy seedless orange slices, and crisp mixed greens form the base, while crumbled feta or goat cheese adds a creamy contrast. Toasted hazelnuts bring a rich, nutty crunch, tying everything together beautifully. A zesty dressing drizzled over the top enhances the sweet-and-savory balance.

Honey-Orange Dressing (recipe at right)
6 cups lightly packed arugula or other salad greens
3 cups shredded, sliced, or chopped rotisserie chicken or 3 cooked chicken breasts, sliced
2 seedless oranges, peeled, seeded, and sliced
⅓ cup crumbled feta or goat cheese
¼ cup chopped toasted hazelnuts

1. Prepare Honey-Orange Dressing; cover and refrigerate until ready to serve.
2. Divide greens among 4 salad plates and top evenly with chicken. Arrange oranges on top. Sprinkle evenly with cheese and nuts. Shake Honey-Orange Dressing well and drizzle on top.

HONEY-ORANGE DRESSING

½ teaspoon orange zest
⅓ cup fresh orange juice
¼ cup extra-virgin olive oil
2 tablespoons apple cider vinegar
1½ tablespoons honey
¼ teaspoon fine sea salt
¼ teaspoon coarsely ground black pepper

Combine orange zest and juice, olive oil, vinegar, honey, salt, and pepper in a jar. Cover tightly with lid and shake vigorously. Store leftover dressing in the refrigerator for up to 1 week. Makes about ¾ cup.

CHICKEN-AND-GRAIN BOWL WITH CREAMY GREEN GODDESS DRESSING

MAKES 2 SERVINGS

Tender grilled chicken, hearty grains, and a medley of crisp vegetables combine under a creamy, herb-packed yogurt dressing that ties it all together with a burst of freshness in every bite. Perfect for meal prep or a wholesome lunch, this bowl is endlessly customizable—swap the chicken for chickpeas or tofu for a vegetarian twist or mix up the veggies with whatever's in season.

2 cups mixed salad greens
1 cup cooked farro, quinoa, or brown rice
½ cucumber, diced
1 to 2 small tomatoes, cut into wedges
1 avocado, sliced
2 cooked-and-sliced chicken breasts or 2 cups shredded cooked chicken
Creamy Green Goddess Dressing (recipe at right)
Coarsely ground black pepper

Arrange salad greens, farro, cucumber, tomatoes, and avocado evenly in 2 salad bowls. Top with chicken. Drizzle with Creamy Green Goddess Dressing and sprinkle with pepper. Serve with additional dressing.

CREAMY GREEN GODDESS DRESSING

1 cup Greek yogurt
3 tablespoons extra-virgin olive oil
½ teaspoon lemon zest
2 tablespoons lemon juice
1 tablespoon white wine vinegar
1 cup lightly packed fresh parsley
¼ cup lightly packed fresh basil
1 green onion, sliced
1 small garlic clove, minced
¼ teaspoon fine sea salt
¼ teaspoon coarsely ground black pepper

Combine yogurt, oil, lemon zest and juice, vinegar, parsley, basil, green onion, garlic, salt, and pepper in a blender. Blend until smooth, stopping to scrape down sides with a spatula. Store in the refrigerator for up to 3 days. Makes 1½ cups.

SPICY CHICKEN-AND-MANGO SALAD BOWL WITH CILANTRO-LIME VINAIGRETTE

MAKES 4 SERVINGS

This bright, refreshing salad bowl balances smoky, spiced chicken with the sweetness of ripe mango, all tied together with a zesty vinaigrette. This is a great way to repurpose leftover chicken into a satisfying and vibrant meal. Serve it as a light lunch or a colorful dinner option that comes together in minutes.

2 ripe mangoes, peeled and diced
1 (15.5-ounce) can black beans, rinsed and drained
½ large red bell pepper, diced
2 tablespoons finely chopped red onion
¼ cup Cilantro-Lime Vinaigrette (recipe at right)
6 cups mixed greens such as romaine, spinach, or arugula
2 cups cooked quinoa
4 packaged grilled or seasoned chicken breasts, sliced

1. Combine mango, black beans, bell pepper, onion, and Cilantro-Lime Vinaigrette in a large bowl.
2. Divide greens among 4 serving bowls. Top each evenly with quinoa and mango mixture. Arrange chicken slices on top. Serve with additional vinaigrette.

CILANTRO-LIME VINAIGRETTE

1 teaspoon grated lime zest
¼ cup fresh lime juice
¼ cup mild extra-virgin olive oil
2 tablespoons rice vinegar
2 tablespoons granulated sugar or honey
1 teaspoon ground cumin
1 teaspoon chili powder
¼ teaspoon fine sea salt
⅛ teaspoon ground cayenne pepper
1 garlic clove, minced
2 tablespoons chopped fresh cilantro

Combine lime zest and juice, oil, vinegar, sugar, cumin, chili powder, salt, cayenne, garlic, and cilantro in a jar. Cover and shake vigorously. Makes ¾ cup.

CHICKEN NOODLE BOWL WITH PEANUT-COCONUT DRESSING

MAKES 4 SERVINGS

This satisfying meal is packed with flavor and crunch. Tender chicken—either from a rotisserie or simply cooked and sliced—sits atop silky rice noodles, crisp red bell peppers, carrots, cucumber, and red onion. Perfect for a quick lunch or light dinner, this dish is easy to prepare and can be customized with fresh herbs, chopped peanuts, or a squeeze of lime for extra brightness.

½ (8-ounce) package rice noodles

3½ cups shredded or chopped rotisserie chicken or 3 cooked chicken breasts, sliced

1 red bell pepper, thinly sliced

1 carrot, julienned or grated

½ seedless cucumber, halved and sliced

¼ red onion, very thinly sliced

Peanut-Coconut Dressing (recipe at right)

1 tablespoon fresh cilantro leaves

1. Soak noodles in hot water to cover for 15 to 20 minutes or until tender; rinse and drain. (For easier serving, cut noodles into pieces with kitchen shears.)

2. Arrange noodles in 4 serving bowls. Top with chicken, bell pepper, carrot, cucumber, and onion. Drizzle with Peanut-Coconut Dressing. Sprinkle with cilantro leaves and additional dressing.

PEANUT-COCONUT DRESSING

This creamy dressing is the star of the show, adding a rich, slightly sweet, and lightly spiced Thai-inspired flavor that ties everything together.

1 cup coconut milk

½ cup creamy peanut butter

1 to 2 tablespoons sriracha or chili-garlic sauce

½ teaspoon grated lime zest

2 tablespoons fresh lime juice

1 tablespoon grated fresh gingerroot

1 teaspoon light brown sugar

2 teaspoons rice vinegar

1 garlic clove, minced

¼ teaspoon fine sea salt

Whisk together coconut milk, peanut butter, sriracha, and lime zest and juice in a bowl. Stir in ginger, brown sugar, vinegar, garlic, and salt. Cover and chill until ready to serve. Store leftovers in the refrigerator for up to 1 week. Makes 1¾ cups.

CHICKEN SALAD BOWL WITH FIVE-SPICE VINAIGRETTE

MAKES 4 SERVINGS

This meal strikes a nice balance of savory, sweet, and crunchy, thanks to the aromatic seasoning and a zesty vinaigrette. Chinese five-spice is a fragrant blend typically featuring star anise, cloves, cinnamon, fennel, and pepper, with occasional additions like ginger, nutmeg, or turmeric. You can substitute other seasoning blends like Mexican, jerk, salt-free—your choice!

1 (6-ounce) package rice noodles
Five-Spice Vinaigrette (recipe at right)
3 cups sliced or shredded romaine lettuce
2 cups baby arugula
¼ cup fresh cilantro leaves
½ English cucumber, sliced
1 cup coarsely shredded carrots
4 large radishes, thinly sliced
4 cooked chicken breasts or 1 pound cooked chicken breast strips

1. Soak noodles in warm or room-temperature water for 10 to 15 minutes or until tender and pliable. Drain and set aside.
2. Prepare Five-Spice Vinaigrette.
3. Divide noodles evenly into 4 serving bowls. Top evenly with lettuces, cilantro, cucumber, carrots, and radishes. Top with chicken. Drizzle vinaigrette evenly over salad.

FIVE-SPICE VINAIGRETTE

3 tablespoons lime juice
2 tablespoons extra-virgin olive oil
1 tablespoon rice vinegar
1 tablespoon water
1 teaspoon sriracha sauce
½ teaspoon honey
1 tablespoon soy sauce
2 teaspoons Chinese five-spice powder

Whisk together lime juice, oil, vinegar, 1 tablespoon water, sriracha, and honey in a small bowl. Stir in soy sauce and five-spice powder. Makes ½ cup.

CHICKEN BURRITO BOWL WITH CREAMY CHIPOTLE DRESSING

MAKES 2 LARGE SERVINGS

This hearty bowl is packed with protein! If you prefer a vinaigrette style dressing, the Smoky Cumin Vinaigrette (page 136) is a delicious option.

2 tablespoons extra-virgin olive oil
1 tablespoon lime juice
½ teaspoon chili powder
½ teaspoon cumin
¼ teaspoon garlic powder
¼ teaspoon paprika
¼ teaspoon coarsely ground black pepper
2 cups shredded rotisserie chicken
1 (15-ounce) can black beans, rinsed and drained
¾ cup corn kernels (fresh, canned, or frozen)
½ cup cherry tomatoes, halved
2 tablespoons red onion, cut into slivers or diced
1 avocado, sliced or diced
2 small heads romaine lettuce, sliced or chopped
1 cup cooked yellow rice (store-bought or leftover)
¼ cup shredded cheddar or Monterey Jack cheese
1 tablespoon fresh cilantro, chopped
Creamy Chipotle Dressing (recipe at right)

1. Combine oil, lime juice, chili powder, cumin, garlic powder, paprika, and black pepper in a large bowl. Stir in chicken, beans, corn, tomatoes, and onion, tossing to coat. Add avocado, tossing gently.

2. Divide lettuce among 2 large salad bowls. Top evenly with rice, then chicken mixture. Sprinkle evenly with cheese and cilantro. Drizzle with Creamy Chipotle Dressing and serve with additional dressing.

CREAMY CHIPOTLE DRESSING

½ cup sour cream
1 tablespoon mayonnaise
1 tablespoon lime juice
1 teaspoon chipotle peppers in adobo sauce, finely chopped
1 teaspoon adobo sauce (from can of chipotle peppers)
½ teaspoon garlic powder
¼ teaspoon cumin
¼ teaspoon smoked paprika
1 tablespoon water (plus more to thin as needed)

Combine sour cream, mayonnaise, lime juice, chipotle peppers, adobo sauce, garlic powder, cumin, and paprika in a bowl, stirring until well blended. Add 1 tablespoon water, plus more, if necessary, to obtain a pourable consistency. Makes about ¾ cup.

GREEK CHICKEN RICE BOWL WITH TZATZIKI DRESSING

MAKES 4 SERVINGS

This flavorful rice bowl is excellent for a quick lunch or dinner. Using store-bought rotisserie or precooked chicken, this dish comes together in no time.

3 cups red and green leaf lettuce
3 cups cooked basmati or jasmine rice
¼ cup extra-virgin olive oil
½ teaspoon lemon zest
1 tablespoon lemon juice
1 tablespoon chopped fresh or ½ teaspoon dried oregano
¼ teaspoon garlic powder
¼ teaspoon paprika
¼ teaspoon fine sea salt
¼ teaspoon coarsely ground black pepper
2½ cups shredded rotisserie chicken or any precooked chicken
1 cup cherry tomatoes, halved
½ seedless cucumber, diced
8 Kalamata olives, halved
¼ cup feta cheese, crumbled
Tzatziki Dressing (recipe at right)

1. Divide lettuce evenly among 4 salad bowls.
2. Combine rice, olive oil, lemon zest and juice, oregano, garlic powder, paprika, salt, and pepper in a large bowl, stirring until well blended. Spoon about ¾ cup rice into each bowl. Top evenly with chicken.
3. Arrange tomatoes, cucumber, and olives around chicken. Sprinkle with feta and drizzle with Tzatziki Dressing.

TZATZIKI DRESSING

This creamy dressing brings fresh Mediterranean flavors to every bite.

½ seedless cucumber
½ cup Greek yogurt
1 tablespoon lemon juice
1 tablespoon extra-virgin olive oil
1 teaspoon fresh or ½ teaspoon dried dill
1 small clove garlic, minced
¼ teaspoon fine sea salt
¼ teaspoon coarsely ground black pepper
1 to 2 tablespoons water (optional)

1. Grate cucumber coarsely and drain in a fine wire-mesh sieve placed over a bowl; let stand for 15 minutes. Press down with a spoon or spatula to squeeze out excess liquid.
2. Combine yogurt, lemon juice, oil, dill, garlic, salt, and pepper in a bowl, stirring until well blended. Stir in drained cucumber. Add 1 to 2 tablespoons water, if desired, to obtain a pourable consistency. Makes 1¼ cups.

ZA'ATAR CHICKEN, BULGUR, AND LENTIL SALAD BOWL

MAKES 4 SERVINGS

2 cups cooked-and-cooled bulgur, farro, or quinoa

1 cup cooked brown or green lentils

1 cup firmly packed fresh parsley, finely chopped

¼ cup fresh mint leaves, chopped

2 tablespoons extra-virgin olive oil

2 tablespoons fresh lemon juice

1 tablespoon za'atar or Moroccan seasoning blend

⅛ teaspoon fine sea salt

1 cup cherry tomatoes, halved

½ seedless cucumber, chopped

3 tablespoons finely chopped red onion

¼ cup crumbled feta cheese

3 cups shredded rotisserie or grilled chicken breast

¼ cup toasted pine nuts or slivered almonds (optional)

Lemon-Tahini Dressing (page 145)

This high-protein salad is packed with earthy flavors and interesting textures. Fresh herbs, crisp vegetables, and a lemony tahini dressing bring it all together. For a lighter flavor, substitute Honey-Orange Dressing (page 126).

1. Combine bulgur, lentils, parsley, and mint in a bowl. Stir together oil, lemon juice, seasoning blend, and salt in a small bowl. Stir into bulgur mixture. Stir in tomatoes, cucumber, onion, and feta.

2. Divide mixture evenly among 4 salad bowls. Top with chicken and nuts, if desired. Drizzle with Lemon-Tahini Dressing and serve with additional dressing.

SALAD BOWL WITH CURRIED MISO DRESSING

MAKES 2 SERVINGS

Leftover grilled chicken and precooked rice or quinoa makes this dish quick to assemble. Slices of baked tofu make a delicious vegetarian option.

2 cups mixed chopped salad greens

1 cup thinly sliced red cabbage

¼ cup lightly packed fresh cilantro leaves

2 carrots, shredded

1 cup cooked rice, quinoa, or other grain*

1 avocado, sliced

½ cucumber, quartered and sliced

¼ cup shelled edamame (optional)

6 ounces cooked chicken breast, sliced, or 6 ounces baked tofu, sliced or cubed

1 tablespoon toasted sesame seeds (optional)

Curried Miso Dressing (recipe at right)

Combine greens, cabbage, cilantro, and carrots in a large bowl, tossing until blended. Arrange on 2 salad plates. Top evenly with rice; avocado slices; cucumber; and, if desired, edamame. Top evenly with chicken or tofu. Sprinkle with toasted sesame seeds, if desired. Drizzle with Curried Miso Dressing and serve with additional dressing.

* I've tried this with 1 (8.5-ounce) package precooked Chinese five-spice grain medley such as Ben's Original. It's not very common in stores, so substitute any seasoned rice or make your own quinoa or grain blend.

CURRIED MISO DRESSING

¼ cup white miso paste

¼ cup water

2 tablespoons rice wine vinegar

1 teaspoon grated or finely minced fresh ginger

1 small garlic clove, chopped

1 teaspoon curry powder

¼ teaspoon coarsely ground black pepper

¼ cup extra-virgin olive oil

1 tablespoon chopped fresh chives

Combine miso, ¼ cup water, vinegar, ginger, garlic, curry powder, and pepper in a blender. Blend well. With blender running, drizzle olive oil into mixture in a thin stream. Stir in chives. Makes ¾ cup.

STEAK, CORN, AND TOMATO SALAD WITH SMOKY CUMIN VINAIGRETTE

MAKES 4 SERVINGS

This cheerful Tex-Mex-inspired salad is packed with flavor and fresh ingredients. Instead of cooking a steak from scratch, I turn to thinly sliced deli roast beef for convenience. Use kernels from leftover corn on the cob, or opt for fire-roasted corn for additional flavor. Multicolor tortilla strips, found in the salad area of the produce section, add a nice crunchy texture.

8 cups chopped romaine lettuce or mixed greens

½ pound deli roast beef, sliced into thin strips

1 cup cherry tomatoes, halved

1 cup fresh or frozen-and-thawed corn kernels

1 avocado, diced or sliced

½ cup black beans, rinsed and drained

¼ cup thinly sliced red onion

¼ cup chopped fresh cilantro

Smoky Cumin Vinaigrette (recipe at right)

½ cup crumbled cotija, queso fresco, or feta cheese

½ cup packaged tortilla strips

Arrange lettuce, roast beef, tomatoes, corn, avocado, black beans, onion, and cilantro on a large salad platter or on individual plates. Drizzle with Smoky Cumin Vinaigrette. Sprinkle with cheese and tortilla strips. Serve with additional vinaigrette.

SMOKY CUMIN VINAIGRETTE

Smoked paprika in the vinaigrette adds a rich, outdoorsy flavor to the dressing, but plain paprika works well too.

¼ cup extra-virgin olive oil

½ teaspoon lime zest

2 tablespoons lime juice

1½ tablespoons red wine vinegar

1 teaspoon honey or agave syrup

1 teaspoon ground cumin

¼ to ½ teaspoon smoked paprika

½ teaspoon chili powder

¼ teaspoon garlic powder

¼ teaspoon fine sea salt

¼ teaspoon coarsely ground black pepper

Combine oil, lime zest and juice, vinegar, honey, cumin, paprika, chili powder, garlic powder, salt, and pepper in a jar. Tighten lid and shake vigorously. Makes ½ cup.

BEEFSTEAK SALAD WITH BLUE CHEESE-BALSAMIC VINAIGRETTE

MAKES 4 SERVINGS

This no-cook salad is a perfect solution for busy days when you want something hearty yet effortless. Deli-sliced roast beef pairs beautifully with juicy tomatoes, all tied together with a tangy vinaigrette. The blend of savory, creamy, and bright flavors makes this dish feel indulgent. Serve it as a quick lunch, a light dinner, or an elegant appetizer with crusty bread on the side.

8 cups torn mixed greens or green leaf lettuce, torn

12 to 16 ounces rare roast beef, shaved, sliced, or cut into strips

4 small ripe tomatoes, cut into wedges

4 thin slices red onion

Blue Cheese-Balsamic Vinaigrette (recipe at right)

⅓ cup chopped toasted pecans

Coarsely ground black pepper

Arrange greens, beef, tomatoes, and onion on 4 serving plates. Drizzle with Blue Cheese-Balsamic Vinaigrette, and sprinkle with pecans and pepper.

BLUE CHEESE-BALSAMIC VINAIGRETTE

3 tablespoons white balsamic vinegar

1 tablespoon water

1 teaspoon Dijon mustard

½ cup extra-virgin olive oil

½ teaspoon fine sea salt

½ teaspoon coarsely ground black pepper

¼ cup crumbled blue cheese

Combine vinegar, 1 tablespoon water, mustard, oil, salt, and pepper in a jar. Cover and shake vigorously. Add cheese; cover and shake vigorously. Makes ¾ cup.

ROAST BEEF SALAD WITH HEIRLOOM TOMATOES AND THAI DRESSING

MAKES 4 SERVINGS

This vibrant mix of fresh vegetables and herbs is brought to life with a bold dressing that includes fish sauce for its signature umami depth. The balance of sweet, sour, salty, and spicy makes this salad a standout side or light main dish.

6 cups torn romaine lettuce

¼ cup lightly packed fresh cilantro, chopped

¼ cup lightly packed fresh mint, chopped

¼ cup lightly packed fresh Thai basil (optional)

8 ounces thickly sliced rare deli roast beef, cut into wide strips

½ large seedless cucumber, halved and sliced

2 large heirloom tomatoes, cut into wedges

⅓ cup coarsely chopped seasoned or plain roasted cashews or peanuts

Thai Dressing (recipe at right)

1. Combine romaine; cilantro; mint; and, if desired, basil in a large bowl. Arrange lettuce mixture on a large serving platter or individual plates. Top with beef, cucumber, and tomatoes. Sprinkle with cashews.

2. Drizzle Thai Dressing over salad just before serving.

THAI DRESSING

Fish sauce adds a salty, savory punch, but if you're new to its flavor, it's perfectly fine to start with half the amount and adjust to taste. For those who love heat, finely chopped red chilies can be stirred directly into the dressing, allowing their spice to infuse every bite. Adjust the amount based on your spice tolerance, or serve them on the side for a customizable kick.

1 shallot, minced

¼ teaspoon lime zest

¼ cup fresh lime juice

2 tablespoons Asian fish sauce

1 tablespoon dark brown sugar

1 red Thai or serrano chili, thinly sliced (seeded, if desired)

Whisk together shallot, lime zest and juice, fish sauce, and brown sugar in a small bowl. Stir in sliced chili. Let stand for 15 to 30 minutes to let flavors marry. Makes about ½ cup.

WATERCRESS-AND-ROAST BEEF SALAD WITH CHIMICHURRI VINAIGRETTE

MAKES 4 SERVINGS

The star of this dish is its lovely chimichurri vinaigrette, which adds a fresh, garlicky punch to the hearty salad and perfectly complements the richness of the beef.

4 cups watercress, trimmed

2 to 3 large heirloom tomatoes, sliced

12 ounces deli-sliced roast beef or leftover grilled skirt steak, thinly sliced

Chimichurri Vinaigrette (recipe at right)

Arrange watercress, tomatoes, and roast beef on a large platter or individual salad plates. Drizzle with Chimichurri Vinaigrette and serve with additional vinaigrette.

CHIMICHURRI VINAIGRETTE

½ cup packed fresh Italian parsley

1 teaspoon fresh oregano leaves

½ to 1 large garlic clove

⅛ teaspoon lime zest

1 tablespoon fresh lime juice

1 tablespoon red wine vinegar

1 tablespoon water

1 teaspoon granulated sugar

¾ teaspoon ground cumin

½ teaspoon ground chili powder

⅛ teaspoon crushed red pepper flakes

¼ cup extra-virgin olive oil

Combine parsley, oregano, garlic, lime zest and juice, vinegar, 1 tablespoon water, sugar, cumin, chili powder, and red pepper flakes in a blender or small food processor. Process until very finely chopped. With blender running, drizzle in oil. Makes ½ cup.

HEARTY CUBAN SALAD WITH MOJO VINAIGRETTE

MAKES 4 SERVINGS

This entrée salad is a perfect way to repurpose leftover grilled steak, grilled chicken, or shredded rotisserie chicken—or use a mix for variety.

1 (4-ounce) container watercress

½ (5-ounce) container arugula or other salad greens

3 cups leftover sliced grilled steak or chicken or shredded rotisserie chicken

2 jarred roasted red bell peppers, cut into strips

1 avocado, sliced

1 cup grape or cherry tomatoes, halved

¼ red onion, thinly sliced

⅓ cup crumbled feta or cotija cheese

Mojo Vinaigrette (recipe at right)

Divide watercress and greens on a large platter or individual serving plates. Top evenly with meat, bell peppers, avocado, tomatoes, onion, and cheese. Drizzle with Mojo Vinaigrette and serve with additional vinaigrette.

MOJO VINAIGRETTE

This citrusy dressing brightens salads with just the right amount of tropical, cheerful flair.

1 green onion, cut into pieces

2 garlic cloves, coarsely chopped

¼ cup orange juice

2 tablespoons lime juice

1 tablespoon lemon juice

⅓ cup extra-virgin olive oil

1 teaspoon fresh oregano leaves

1 teaspoon granulated sugar or honey

½ teaspoon ground cumin

½ teaspoon fine sea salt

¼ teaspoon coarsely ground black pepper

Combine onion, garlic, juices, oil, oregano, sugar, cumin, salt, and pepper in a small food processor. Pulse until well blended. Makes ¾ cup.

ANTIPASTO SALAD WITH MARINATED ARTICHOKES, BEANS, SLIVERED MEATS, AND CREAMY HUMMUS DRESSING

MAKES 6 SERVINGS

To reduce sodium or fat, substitute plain ripe olives and sliced deli turkey. This salad is also good with Basic Red Wine Vinaigrette (page 68).

- 1 (15-ounce) can cannellini beans or chickpeas, rinsed and drained
- 1 (12-ounce) jar marinated artichoke hearts, drained and chopped
- 1 roasted red bell pepper, sliced into short strips
- ½ cup cherry tomatoes, halved
- ¼ cup mixed pitted olives (ripe black, Kalamata, or green)
- ¼ cup thinly sliced red onion
- 2 ounces salami (about 12 slices), halved
- 2 ounces prosciutto (about 4 slices), sliced
- ¼ cup (1 ounce) shredded or slivered mozzarella or provolone cheese
- Creamy Hummus Dressing (recipe at right)
- 6 cups mixed salad greens
- ¼ cup chopped fresh basil or small basil leaves

1. Combine beans, artichoke hearts, bell pepper, tomatoes, olives, onion, salami, prosciutto, and cheese in a large bowl. Add about ¼ cup Creamy Hummus Dressing, tossing to coat.
2. Place greens in a large salad bowl or platter or divide among individual salad plates. Top with bean mixture and sprinkle with basil. Serve with additional dressing.

CREAMY HUMMUS DRESSING

- ½ cup garlic or plain hummus
- 2 tablespoons extra-virgin olive oil
- 1 tablespoon red wine vinegar
- 1 tablespoon lemon juice
- 1 teaspoon Dijon mustard
- 1 garlic clove, minced
- ½ teaspoon dried oregano or Italian seasoning
- ¼ teaspoon fine sea salt
- ¼ teaspoon coarsely ground black pepper
- 2 to 4 tablespoons water

Whisk together hummus, oil, vinegar, lemon juice, mustard, garlic, oregano, salt, and pepper in a small bowl. Whisk in 2 to 4 tablespoons water to obtain a pourable consistency. Makes ¾ cup.

TUNA NIÇOISE SALAD WITH CAPER-SHALLOT VINAIGRETTE

MAKES 4 SERVINGS

Salad Niçoise is a French dish that usually includes boiled potatoes. If you have leftover boiled baby potatoes, cut them in half and include them. Pickled green beans are a fun, crunchy addition to the standard, but you can also use frozen-and-thawed haricots verts.

6 cups chopped baby romaine or other lettuce
12 to 16 pickled or frozen-and-thawed green beans
2 (6-ounce) cans skipjack or other tuna, drained
⅔ cup yellow or red grape or pear tomatoes, halved
12 Kalamata olives, halved
½ red onion, very thinly sliced
4 hard-boiled eggs, sliced
Caper-Shallot Vinaigrette (recipe at right)

Arrange lettuce evenly on 4 salad plates. Divide beans, tuna, tomatoes, olives, onion, and eggs evenly over lettuce. Drizzle with Caper-Shallot Vinaigrette and serve with additional vinaigrette.

CAPER-SHALLOT VINAIGRETTE

⅔ cup extra-virgin olive oil
¼ cup Champagne or white wine vinegar
1½ teaspoons Dijon mustard
1 shallot, minced
½ teaspoon grated lemon zest
2 tablespoons fresh lemon juice
1 tablespoon capers, coarsely chopped
1 teaspoon Worcestershire sauce
½ teaspoon granulated sugar
¼ teaspoon coarsely ground black pepper

Combine oil, vinegar, mustard, shallot, lemon zest and juice, capers, Worcestershire, sugar, and pepper in a jar. Tighten lid and shake vigorously. Makes 1 cup.

FALL GREENS WITH SMOKED TROUT, PEAR, CRANBERRY, AND DATE VINAIGRETTE

MAKES 4 SERVINGS

This autumn-inspired salad balances sweetness, crunch, and freshness in every bite. Smoked trout is found in markets near the seafood counter, along with smoked salmon and crab. If unavailable, substitute shredded rotisserie chicken or leftover grilled chicken slices.

6 cups baby arugula, red or green leaf lettuce, or a mix

1 large ripe pear or apple, thinly sliced

2 tablespoons thinly sliced red onion

8 ounces smoked trout, skin removed and flaked

⅓ cup crumbled goat cheese or shaved Parmesan

¼ cup toasted pumpkin seeds, pecans, or walnuts

¼ cup dried cranberries or pomegranate arils

Date Vinaigrette (recipe at right)

Arrange greens on a large salad platter or individual dishes. Top evenly with pear and onion. Top evenly with smoked trout. Sprinkle with goat cheese, pumpkin seeds, and cranberries. Drizzle with Date Vinaigrette and serve with additional vinaigrette.

DATE VINAIGRETTE

5 dates, pitted and chopped

⅓ cup warm water

¼ cup apple cider vinegar or white balsamic vinegar

2 teaspoons Dijon mustard

⅓ cup extra-virgin olive oil

¼ teaspoon fine sea salt

⅛ teaspoon coarsely ground black pepper

¼ teaspoon ground cinnamon or allspice

Combine dates and ⅓ cup warm water in a small bowl and let sit for 5 minutes to soften. Transfer to a blender or mini food processor. Add vinegar, mustard, oil, salt, pepper, and cinnamon. Blend until smooth and creamy. Makes ¾ cup.

SMOKED SOCKEYE CAESAR SALAD WITH LEMONY DRESSING

MAKES 2 SERVINGS

Hot smoked salmon brings a rich, flaky texture and deep smoky flavor to this twist on a classic Caesar salad. Unlike cold-smoked salmon, which remains silky and delicate, hot-smoked salmon is fully cooked, making it perfect for flaking into salads. Its bold, savory taste pairs beautifully with crisp romaine, crunchy croutons, and a creamy dressing brightened with lemon zest.

2 romaine lettuce hearts, torn

Lemony Dressing (recipe at right)

4 ounces hot smoked sockeye or other wild salmon

⅓ cup freshly shaved Parmesan cheese

¼ teaspoon coarsely ground black pepper

Store-bought or homemade toasted croutons (optional)

Toss lettuce in just enough Lemony Dressing to lightly coat greens; divide evenly onto 4 plates. Break salmon into pieces, discarding skin. Place evenly on lettuce, and sprinkle with Parmesan and pepper. Top with croutons, if desired. Serve with additional dressing.

LEMONY DRESSING

This dressing, made from scratch with simple ingredients, adds a tangy, garlicky richness that complements smoky fish.

½ cup extra-virgin olive oil

1 teaspoon lemon zest

¼ cup fresh lemon juice

2 teaspoons Worcestershire sauce

2 teaspoons Dijon mustard

½ teaspoon anchovy paste (optional)

1 small garlic clove, grated or finely minced

¼ teaspoon fine sea salt

¼ teaspoon coarsely ground black pepper

½ cup freshly grated Parmesan cheese

Combine oil; lemon zest and juice; Worcestershire; mustard; anchovy paste, if desired; garlic; salt; and pepper in a blender. Blend on high until smooth, stopping to scrape down sides. Add cheese and blend until finely chopped and well blended. Makes 1 cup.

QUINOA-AND-SMOKED SALMON KALE BOWL WITH LEMON-TAHINI DRESSING

MAKES 4 SERVINGS

Some salad bowls feel like a side dish, but this one holds its own as a hearty, protein-packed meal. The creamy dressing ties everything together.

4 cups chopped kale (stems removed)

1 tablespoon extra-virgin olive oil

¼ teaspoon fine sea salt

¼ teaspoon coarsely ground black pepper

2 cups cooked quinoa

1 (15-ounce) can chickpeas, rinsed and drained

2 medium-size carrots, shredded or julienned

Lemon-Tahini Dressing (recipe at right)

4 to 6 ounces hot smoked sockeye salmon

1. Combine kale, oil, salt, and pepper in a large bowl. Massage with hands until leaves soften slightly. Stir in quinoa, chickpeas, and carrots. Drizzle with about ¼ cup Lemon-Tahini Dressing, tossing until lightly coated.

2. Divide quinoa mixture among 4 salad plates or bowls. Remove skin from salmon, break into bite-size pieces, and arrange evenly on salad. Serve with additional dressing.

LEMON-TAHINI DRESSING

¼ cup tahini

½ teaspoon grated lemon zest

2½ tablespoons fresh lemon juice

2 tablespoons tamari or soy sauce

1 tablespoon extra-virgin olive oil

1 tablespoon honey or maple syrup

½ teaspoon minced garlic

¼ teaspoon fine sea salt

⅛ teaspoon cayenne pepper

1 to 2 tablespoons warm water

Combine tahini, lemon zest and juice, tamari, oil, honey, garlic, salt, and cayenne in a bowl, whisking until smooth. Add 1 to 2 tablespoons water to obtain a pourable consistency. Makes ¾ cup.

SMOKED SALMON-AND-BEET SALAD WITH GRIBICHE DRESSING

MAKES 4 SERVINGS

This hearty salad combines the rich flavor of hard-smoked sockeye or coho salmon with sweet roasted beets and peppery greens like arugula. A creamy, protein-rich, hard-boiled-egg dressing tops it all off, adding depth and richness.

6 cups baby arugula or spring lettuces

1 (8-ounce) package refrigerated cooked beets, cut into wedges

2 (4-ounce) hot smoked sockeye salmon filets (plain or cracked black pepper flavored)

⅓ cup toasted pistachios or walnuts, chopped

⅓ cup crumbled feta cheese

Gribiche Dressing (recipe at right)

Arrange lettuce on 4 salad plates. Top evenly with beets and salmon. Sprinkle with nuts and cheese. Drizzle with Gribiche Dressing and serve with additional dressing.

GRIBICHE DRESSING

¼ cup extra-virgin olive oil

2 tablespoons Champagne or white wine vinegar

1 teaspoon Dijon or coarse-ground mustard

1 small shallot, minced

2 teaspoons chopped fresh dill

1 teaspoon capers, rinsed and drained

¼ teaspoon fine sea salt

¼ teaspoon coarsely ground black pepper

2 hard-boiled eggs

1. Whisk together oil, vinegar, mustard, shallot, dill, capers, salt, and pepper in a medium-size bowl.

2. Cut eggs in half. Scoop out egg yolks, crumble finely, and stir into oil mixture. Finely chop egg whites and stir into dressing. Makes 1 cup.

CALIFORNIA ROLL BOWL

MAKES 4 SERVINGS

2 tablespoons rice vinegar

2 teaspoons granulated sugar

3 cups cooked white rice

½ seedless cucumber or 2 miniature cucumbers, diced or sliced

2 large carrots, peeled and julienned or shredded

1 (9-ounce) package shelled edamame, rinsed and drained

1 large avocado, diced or sliced

¼ cup fresh cilantro leaves

1 (8-ounce) package imitation crab, sliced or chopped

Dynamite Sauce (recipe at right)

Garnish: fresh chopped chives

This dish captures all the fresh flavors of the classic sushi roll in a deconstructed way. It features cooked rice, creamy avocado, crisp cucumber, and imitation crab—a budget-friendly alternative to seafood that still delivers great flavor. Use cooked shrimp or leftover grilled salmon for an elevated version.

1. Stir together vinegar and sugar in a large bowl. Add rice, stirring until well blended.

2. Stir in cucumber, carrots, edamame, avocado, and cilantro. Divide mixture evenly among 4 bowls. Top evenly with imitation crab and drizzle with Dynamite Sauce. Garnish, if desired.

Dynamite Sauce: Combine **½ cup mayonnaise, 2 tablespoons sriracha sauce,** and **2 tablespoons low-sodium tamari or soy sauce** in a medium-size bowl, stirring until well blended. Cover and refrigerate for up to 1 week. Makes ¾ cup.

SHRIMP-AND-GLASS NOODLE SALAD

MAKES 4 SERVINGS

½ (8-ounce) package thin rice noodles
½ cup lime juice
¼ cup fish sauce
3 tablespoons light vegetable oil
2 tablespoons rice wine vinegar
2 teaspoons granulated sugar
1 pound cooked medium-size shrimp, peeled and deveined
3 green onions, thinly sliced
2 carrots, julienned or shredded
1 large seedless cucumber, quartered and sliced
1 red bell pepper, cut into strips
¼ cup fresh cilantro leaves, chopped

This Asian salad is a light, refreshing dish bursting with bright lime flavor and savory fish sauce. Crisp cucumber and fresh cilantro add crunch and herbaceous notes, making this salad perfect for warm-weather meals or light lunches. It's made with thin rice noodles—also called cellophane or glass noodles—which have a silky, slippery texture that soaks up the zesty sauce beautifully.

1. Soak noodles in hot water for 10 to 15 minutes or until tender; rinse in cold water and drain. Place in a large mixing bowl. (For easier serving, cut noodles into pieces with kitchen shears.)

2. Combine lime juice, fish sauce, oil, vinegar, and sugar; pour over noodles, tossing to coat. Stir in shrimp, green onions, carrots, cucumber, bell pepper, and cilantro, tossing until well blended. Cover and refrigerate until ready to serve.

SHRIMP-AND-HOPPIN' JOHN SALAD

MAKES 8 CUPS

½ cup extra-virgin olive oil
1 teaspoon fresh lemon zest
¼ cup fresh lemon juice
1 yellow bell pepper, finely chopped
2 celery ribs, finely chopped
½ large sweet onion, finely chopped
1 jalapeño pepper, finely chopped
¼ cup chopped fresh basil
2 tablespoons chopped fresh parsley
1 teaspoon fine sea salt
1 teaspoon coarsely ground black pepper
2 pounds cooked-and-peeled large shrimp
2 (15-ounce) cans black-eyed peas, rinsed and drained
1 cup cooked white rice

Hoppin' John is a Lowcountry dish featuring black-eyed peas and rice that is often eaten on New Year's Day for good luck. This version includes tender large shrimp to create a cool, filling salad. If you have it on hand, add about ¼ cup chopped cooked bacon to the mixture for extra flavor.

1. Stir together oil, lemon zest and juice, bell pepper, celery, onion, jalapeño, basil, parsley, salt, and pepper in an extra-large bowl.
2. Stir in shrimp, black-eyed peas, and rice, tossing until well coated. Cover and chill for several hours before serving.

CRAWFISH RÉMOULADE

MAKES 4 SERVINGS

½ cup mayonnaise
2 tablespoons Creole mustard
1 teaspoon prepared horseradish
1 tablespoon fresh lemon juice
2 teaspoons white wine vinegar
½ teaspoon hot sauce (or to taste)
¼ teaspoon paprika
¼ teaspoon garlic powder
4 green onions, finely chopped
1 rib celery, finely chopped
1 tablespoon chopped fresh parsley
¼ teaspoon coarsely ground black pepper
12 ounces cooked, peeled crawfish tails, thawed and drained well if frozen
½ head Bibb lettuce, leaves separated, rinsed, and patted dry
Garnish: fresh parsley sprigs

> Invite a few close friends over to your house for a chic lunch. They'll be delighted when you serve this impressive dish that only looks like you've spent hours in the kitchen!

This Southern classic dish highlights tender crawfish tails tossed in a creamy dressing. The bold flavors of Creole mustard, horseradish, and hot sauce balance beautifully with the sweetness of the crawfish. Serve it over crisp Bibb lettuce for a refreshing starter or a light lunch that's full of Louisiana flair. Crawfish are harvested fresh in the spring, although they are found frozen year-round. You can easily substitute small- to medium-size peeled-and-deveined shrimp or langostino tails, if desired. Serve over lettuce for a salad or in buns for a sandwich.

1. In a medium-size bowl, whisk together mayonnaise, mustard, horseradish, lemon juice, vinegar, hot sauce, paprika, and garlic powder until smooth. Stir in green onions, celery, parsley, and pepper.
2. Fold in crawfish tails and mix gently until evenly coated. Cover and chill for at least 30 minutes to let flavors marry.
3. Arrange lettuce leaves on individual plates and top evenly with crawfish mixture. Garnish, if desired. Serve cold.

DESSERTS

154 No-Churn Mixed-Berry Ice Cream
155 Super Quick-and-Easy Peach Sherbet
156 Chocolate-Hazelnut Ice Cream
157 Chocolate Brownie-Batter Hummus
158 Tiramisu
159 Strawberry-Brownie Trifle Cups
160 Raspberry-and-Lemon Icebox Cake
162 Berry-Cheesecake Cups
163 No-Bake Chocolate Cheesecake with Chocolate Cookie Crust
164 Gingersnap-and-Berries Tart
165 Lemon Icebox Pie
166 No-Bake Banana Cream Pie with Chocolate Layer
167 Frozen Peanut Butter Pie
168 Possum Pie
170 Chocolate-Covered Pecan Pie Balls
171 No-Bake Chocolate-Topped Peanut Butter-Oat Cups
172 Raw Pecan-and-Date Brownies

164

154

171

165

NO-CHURN MIXED-BERRY ICE CREAM

MAKES 7 CUPS

2 cups mixed berries (strawberries, raspberries, blueberries, blackberries—fresh or frozen and partially thawed)

1 tablespoon lemon juice

1 (14-ounce) can sweetened condensed milk

2 teaspoons vanilla extract

2 cups cold heavy cream

This summer lifesaver requires no stove, no ice-cream machine, and no fuss. Just blend, whip, and freeze! The magic lies in the combination of sweetened condensed milk and whipped cream, which creates a creamy, scoopable texture without the need for churning. Pureed berries bring color and bold, fruity flavor. I like to strain the puree for a silky finish, but you can leave the seeds in for a little texture and a more rustic vibe.

1. Combine berries and lemon juice in a food processor. Process until smooth. If desired, strain through a fine wire-mesh sieve to remove seeds.

2. Whisk together condensed milk and vanilla in a large bowl. Stir in berry puree.

3. Beat heavy cream in a mixing bowl with an electric mixer until stiff peaks form. Gently fold whipped cream into berry mixture until well combined.

4. Pour ice-cream mixture into a large loaf pan or 8-cup freezer-safe container. Smooth top and cover with plastic wrap or a lid. Freeze for at least 6 hours or until firm. Scoop and enjoy!

SUPER QUICK-AND-EASY PEACH SHERBET

MAKES 4 CUPS

1 (1-pound) package frozen sliced peaches
1 cup plain Greek yogurt
½ cup granulated sugar
½ cup orange juice
½ teaspoon vanilla extract
Garnish: fresh mint sprigs

This dreamy, creamy treat comes together in minutes, thanks to the magic of frozen peaches. Blended with tangy Greek yogurt, a splash of orange juice, and just a hint of vanilla, it delivers the perfect balance of sweet and tart. Keep a bag of frozen peeled peaches in the freezer and you'll always be only moments away from a refreshing, fruit-forward dessert—no ice-cream maker needed.

1. Combine peaches, yogurt, sugar, orange juice, and vanilla in a food processor. Process until very smooth.
2. Pour mixture into an 8- or 9-inch square baking pan. Freeze for several hours or until firm. Scoop mixture into bowls just before serving. Garnish, if desired.

CHOCOLATE-HAZELNUT ICE CREAM

MAKES 6 SERVINGS

1 (7.7-ounce) jar chocolate-hazelnut spread such as Nutella

½ cup granulated sugar

2 cups heavy whipping cream

1 teaspoon vanilla extract

⅛ teaspoon fine sea salt

This rich, no-cook treat is a dream for anyone craving a decadent frozen treat with minimal prep. Made with just a handful of ingredients and churned in an ice-cream maker, the result is ultra-smooth with that signature chocolate-hazelnut flavor in every bite. Churning incorporates air and keeps ice crystals small, creating a silky texture that can't be achieved by simply freezing a mixture. It's the perfect make-ahead dessert—easy, indulgent, and always a hit.

1. Combine chocolate-hazelnut spread, sugar, cream, vanilla, and salt in a blender. Blend until smooth and creamy. Store in the refrigerator until ready to churn.

2. Pour mixture into an ice-cream maker and process according to manufacturer's instructions. Transfer ice cream to an airtight container and freeze for 2 hours or until firm and scoopable.

CHOCOLATE BROWNIE-BATTER HUMMUS

MAKES ABOUT 2 CUPS

1 (15-ounce) can chickpeas, rinsed and drained
¼ cup unsweetened cocoa powder
¼ cup maple syrup
¼ cup almond butter
¼ cup almond milk or water
1 teaspoon vanilla extract
Pinch of fine sea salt
Garnish: grated chocolate
Sugar cookies

This rich, chocolaty hummus is a surprisingly wholesome treat. Made with canned chickpeas, cocoa powder, and maple syrup, it blends into a silky-smooth dip that tastes like decadent brownie batter but offers the plant-based benefits of hummus. Enjoy it with sugar cookies, fresh fruit, pretzels, or graham crackers—or just grab a big spoon!

Combine chickpeas, cocoa powder, maple syrup, almond butter, almond milk, vanilla, and salt in a food processor. Blend until smooth, scraping down sides periodically with a spatula. For more sweetness, add 1 tablespoon maple syrup. Garnish, if desired; serve with sugar cookies.

TIRAMISU

MAKES 8 SERVINGS

2 (8-ounce) containers mascarpone cheese

1¼ cups heavy whipping cream

¼ cup powdered sugar

2 teaspoons vanilla extract

1 cup espresso or very strong coffee, cooled to room temperature

2 tablespoons coffee liqueur or dark rum

2 (3-ounce) packages ladyfingers, divided

2 ounces bittersweet or dark chocolate, grated and divided

Tiramisu is a beloved Italian dessert known for its layers of espresso-soaked ladyfingers and creamy mascarpone filling, dusted with grated chocolate or cocoa powder for a pretty finishing touch. This version uses mascarpone cheese for richness, but you can substitute full-fat cream cheese blended with a little heavy cream for a similar result. The dessert is typically made with a splash of liqueur, but it's just as delicious with extra espresso for an alcohol-free version. Best served chilled, tiramisu is easy to make ahead and always a crowd favorite.

1. Combine mascarpone, whipping cream, powdered sugar, and vanilla in a large bowl. Beat at high speed with an electric mixer until smooth and well blended. Set aside.

2. Stir together espresso and liqueur in a bowl.

3. Arrange half of ladyfingers in bottom of a 9x9-inch baking dish. Brush with half of espresso mixture and spread with half of mascarpone mixture. Sprinkle with half of grated chocolate. Repeat layers with remaining half of ladyfingers, espresso mixture, mascarpone mixture, and chocolate.

4. Cover and chill for several hours or until firm.

STRAWBERRY-BROWNIE TRIFLE CUPS

MAKES 8 SERVINGS

1½ cups whole milk

1 (14-ounce) can sweetened condensed milk

1 (3.4-ounce) package instant vanilla pudding mix

2 teaspoons vanilla extract

1½ cups heavy whipping cream

1 pound baked brownies, broken into pieces and divided

1 (1-pound) package strawberries, sliced and divided

Garnishes: grated semisweet chocolate, additional brownie pieces, sliced strawberries

This dessert is a fun, portable twist on the classic layered dessert, combining yummy brownie chunks, sweet strawberries, and a rich vanilla pudding. Making them in individual cups not only makes serving easier—since the pudding can be a bit messy—but also adds a charming touch for parties or gatherings. For picnics or on-the-go events, canning jars with lids are a perfect solution: They travel well, stack easily, and look great too. Assemble them ahead of time and chill until ready to serve for a stress-free dessert everyone will love. If you need to stretch the dessert to serve more, you can divide it among 12 (9-ounce) clear plastic disposable cups. There is plenty of the luscious vanilla pudding, so you can increase the amount of brownies and strawberries as long as your containers can hold it all.

1. Combine milk, condensed milk, and pudding mix in a large bowl, stirring until smooth and well blended. Stir in vanilla. Cover and chill for 4 hours to overnight or until mixture is firmly set.

2. Beat whipping cream in a mixing bowl with an electric mixer until stiff peaks form. Fold into pudding mixture.

3. Divide half of brownie pieces evenly in bottom of 8 (1½- to 2-cup) jars, containers, or bowls. Top each with about ⅓ cup pudding mixture. Divide half of sliced strawberries evenly over pudding. Repeat with remaining half of brownie pieces, pudding mixture, and strawberries. Garnish, if desired.

RASPBERRY-AND-LEMON ICEBOX CAKE

MAKES 1 (9-INCH) CAKE

Butter or vegetable cooking spray

3 cups heavy whipping cream

1 teaspoon vanilla extract

½ teaspoon almond extract

1 (8-ounce) package cream cheese, softened

¾ cup powdered sugar

½ cup seedless raspberry preserves

15 to 18 graham crackers, divided

2 cups frozen raspberries, divided

6 tablespoons lemon curd, divided

Garnishes: fresh or frozen-and-thawed raspberries, lemon slices

> **This pretty cake has to be made a day ahead, so it takes some planning, but the delicious results are worth it! And though there are several steps, none of them are challenging.**

Bright, creamy, and refreshingly tart, this cake is the perfect no-bake dessert for warm weather or whenever you need a fuss-free sweet treat. A dreamy mixture of cream cheese and whipped cream gets fruity flair from raspberry preserves and lemon curd, layered between crisp graham crackers that soften to a cake-like texture as the dessert sets. Pop it in the fridge for a creamy chill or the freezer for an almost semifreddo-like texture. Either way, it's sliceable sunshine.

1. Using parchment paper, line bottom of a 9-inch springform pan with removable sides. Lightly butter or grease (with cooking spray) sides of pan.

2. Combine whipping cream, vanilla, and almond extract in a large mixing bowl. Beat on medium speed with an electric mixer until foamy; increase speed to high and beat until stiff peaks form.

3. Combine cream cheese, powdered sugar, and raspberry preserves in a mixing bowl. Beat until smooth and well blended. Fold 1 cup whipped cream mixture into raspberry mixture to lighten. Then gradually fold remaining whipped cream mixture into raspberry mixture.

4. Line bottom of prepared pan with 4 or 5 graham crackers, breaking pieces as necessary to completely cover bottom in a single layer.

5. Spread 2 cups raspberry cream evenly over graham crackers. Sprinkle one-third of frozen raspberries on top. Dollop 2 tablespoons lemon curd sporadically over raspberry cream.

6. Repeat layers twice, each with 4 or 5 graham crackers (pressing down firmly), about 2 cups raspberry mixture, one-third of raspberries, and 2 tablespoons lemon curd. Top with remaining raspberry cream.

7. Freeze for 8 to 24 hours or until completely firm. To serve, remove sides of springform pan and transfer cake to a plate or platter. Garnish, if desired.

BERRY-CHEESECAKE CUPS

MAKES 8 SERVINGS

¾ cup finely crushed granola cereal
1 (8-ounce) package cream cheese, softened
1 cup plain Greek yogurt
2 tablespoons honey
2 teaspoons vanilla extract
8 strawberries, sliced
½ cup blueberries

Please your family with minimal effort when you make this dessert. A scoop of prepared granola forms a crunchy, flavorful base—and no oven is required. Creamy cheesecake filling is gently spooned on top and chilled until set, all in cupcake liners for easy handling and portion control. Perfect for parties, lunchboxes, or make-ahead treats, they're simple, portable, and endlessly customizable with your favorite toppings.

1. Place 8 muffin liners in muffin cups. Divide crushed granola evenly into cups, pressing down on bottom.

2. Beat cream cheese in a large mixing bowl until smooth. Stir in yogurt, honey, and vanilla. Divide mixture evenly over granola crust. Cover and refrigerate for 2 to 4 hours or until firm.

3. Top evenly with strawberries and blueberries before serving.

NO-BAKE CHOCOLATE CHEESECAKE WITH CHOCOLATE COOKIE CRUST

MAKES 10 SERVINGS

24 chocolate sandwich cookies such as Oreo cookies (regular, not double-stuffed)

5 tablespoons unsalted butter, melted

8 ounces semisweet or bittersweet chocolate, chopped

2 (8-ounce) packages cream cheese, softened

¾ cup powdered sugar

1 teaspoon vanilla extract

¼ teaspoon fine sea salt

1 cup cold heavy cream

Garnish: chopped chocolate sandwich cookies

Let this cheesecake chill in the fridge until firm, then serve it as-is or top with whipped cream, chocolate curls, or fresh berries for a showstopping finish. I'll make this several days ahead and freeze rather than refrigerate—or I'll freeze leftover slices for a quick treat.

1. Crush cookies (filling included) into fine crumbs using a food processor or by sealing in a zip-top plastic bag and pounding with a rolling pin. Stir in melted butter until mixture resembles wet sand. Press firmly into bottom and slightly up sides of a 9-inch springform pan. Let chill in the refrigerator.

2. Melt the chocolate in a microwave-safe bowl in 30-second intervals, stirring in between, until smooth. Let cool slightly.

3. In a large bowl, beat cream cheese until smooth. Add powdered sugar, vanilla, and salt, and mix until well combined. Stir in melted chocolate until fully incorporated.

4. In a separate bowl, whip cream until stiff peaks form. Fold whipped cream into chocolate mixture in two additions, being careful not to deflate the mixture.

5. Pour filling into prepared crust and smooth top. Garnish, if desired. Cover and refrigerate for at least 6 hours to overnight or until firm.

6. Release from springform pan before serving.

GINGERSNAP-AND-BERRIES TART

MAKES 8 SERVINGS

Gingersnap-Date Crust (recipe at right)
1 (8-ounce) package cream cheese, softened
½ cup firmly packed light brown sugar
⅓ cup sour cream
2 tablespoons lemon juice
1 teaspoon vanilla extract
1 cup fresh raspberries and strawberries
1 cup fresh blackberries
Garnish: fresh mint leaves

This colorful tart features a no-bake crust made from crushed gingersnaps and sweet dates, offering a perfect balance of spicy warmth and natural stickiness to hold it all together. Feel free to substitute my Graham Cracker Crust (page 165). A smooth cream cheese filling with lemon adds a rich, tangy layer, while a colorful topping of fresh berries brings brightness and contrast. I used raspberries and blackberries here but often substitute strawberries and blueberries—use your favorite or what's on sale. I don't use frozen-and-thawed berries in this recipe because they tend to weep juice and thin the filling too much.

1. Prepare Gingersnap-Date Crust and press firmly into an 11-inch tart pan. Let chill in the refrigerator.

2. Beat cream cheese, brown sugar, sour cream, lemon juice, and vanilla in a large bowl until smooth and creamy. Spread evenly into prepared crust. Arrange berries on top. Chill until ready to serve. Garnish, if desired.

Note: It's not easy to cut the tart with the berries on top. You can cut the tart first and then spread berries on each serving. It is also easier to cut slices when the tart is cold.

Gingersnap-Date Crust: Place **2 cups finely crushed gingersnap cookies, 5 pitted dates,** and **4 tablespoons melted salted or unsalted butter** in a food processor. Process until ingredients are well blended and texture resembles wet sand and holds together when pressed. Makes 1 thick crust.

LEMON ICEBOX PIE

MAKES 8 SERVINGS

Graham Cracker Crust (recipe at right)
1 (8-ounce) package cream cheese, softened
1 (14-ounce) can sweetened condensed milk
1 teaspoon grated lemon zest
½ cup fresh lemon juice
Garnishes: whipped cream, lemon slices

This classic Southern favorite brings the ideal balance of flavors, with a smooth, creamy filling nestled in a buttery graham cracker crust. Making the crust from scratch ensures the freshest taste, but if you're short on time, a store-bought crust works just as well. Chilled until firm, this pie is a refreshing treat for warm days—or any time you crave a bright, citrusy dessert with minimal effort.

1. Prepare Graham Cracker Crust; let chill in refrigerator.
2. Combine cream cheese, condensed milk, and lemon zest and juice in a food processor. Process until mixture is creamy and smooth. Pour filling into prepared crust. Refrigerate for 4 hours or until firm. Garnish, if desired.

Graham Cracker Crust: Break **12 graham crackers** into pieces and place in a food processor. Add **2 tablespoons granulated sugar** and **2 tablespoons light brown sugar.** Process until fine crumbs form. Add **6 tablespoons melted salted butter** and process until mixture is well blended and has the texture of wet sand. Transfer crumb mixture to a 9- or 9½-inch pie plate, pressing down firmly on bottom and along sides. Makes 1 crust.

Note: Most graham cracker crusts are baked for a few minutes to brown and firm them up. This version has enough butter that, when chilled, makes a crust that holds together beautifully.

NO-BAKE BANANA CREAM PIE WITH CHOCOLATE LAYER

MAKES 8 SERVINGS

Graham Cracker Crust (page 165)
4 ounces semisweet chocolate, chopped
1 cup plus 3 tablespoons heavy whipping cream, divided
1 (3.4-ounce) box instant vanilla pudding mix
1 cup cold whole milk
2 ripe bananas
2 tablespoons powdered sugar
½ teaspoon vanilla extract
Grated chocolate

This banana cream pie comes together in a snap with a few pantry staples and fresh bananas. Slice the bananas just before layering the ingredients so they do not darken.

1. Assemble Graham Cracker Crust and let chill in the refrigerator.
2. Combine chocolate and 3 tablespoons heavy cream in a small glass bowl. Microwave in 20- to 30-second intervals, stirring each time, until smooth. Spread chocolate mixture over bottom of chilled crust and refrigerate for 10 minutes or until firm.
3. Whisk pudding mix and cold milk in a bowl for about 2 minutes or until smooth and thick.
4. Slice bananas and layer over chocolate mixture. Spread pudding over bananas, smoothing top.
5. Combine remaining 1 cup heavy cream, powdered sugar, and vanilla in a large bowl. Beat until soft peaks form. Spoon or pipe whipped cream over pudding. Sprinkle with grated chocolate. Chill pie in refrigerator for at least 2 hours before serving.

FROZEN PEANUT BUTTER PIE

MAKES 8 SERVINGS

This no-bake pie is rich, creamy, and irresistibly smooth—like a peanut butter cup in pie form! A store-bought crust means there's no oven required—just mix, freeze, and enjoy.

1 cup heavy whipping cream

1 (8-ounce) package cream cheese, softened

⅔ cup creamy peanut butter

½ cup powdered sugar

1 teaspoon vanilla extract

1 (9-inch) prepared chocolate cookie crust, Graham Cracker Crust (page 165), or Graham-Pecan Crust (page 168)

Chocolate Ganache (recipe at right)

Chopped peanuts

1. Beat whipping cream at medium speed with an electric mixer until soft peaks form.

2. Beat cream cheese, peanut butter, powdered sugar, and vanilla in another bowl until creamy and well blended. Fold in whipped cream. Spread peanut butter mixture into piecrust. Freeze for at least 1 hour or until firm.

3. Spread Chocolate Ganache over top. Sprinkle with peanuts. Freeze for at least 1 hour or until firm.

4. Let stand at room temperature for 10 minutes or until thawed enough to slice into servings. (Do not let pie completely thaw or slices will be messy.)

Chocolate Ganache: Combine **½ cup heavy whipping cream** and **6 ounces semisweet chocolate, chopped,** in a microwave-safe bowl. Cook on high in 30-second bursts, stirring occasionally, until chocolate melts. Makes 1 cup.

POSSUM PIE

MAKES 8 TO 10 SERVINGS

Graham-Pecan Crust
  (recipe at right)
1¼ cups heavy cream, divided
½ (8-ounce) package cream cheese, softened
⅓ cup plus 1 tablespoon powdered sugar, divided
1 (3.9-ounce) box instant chocolate pudding mix
1½ cups cold whole milk
¼ teaspoon vanilla extract
Garnish: chocolate shavings

This scrumptious pie will satisfy every sweet tooth in the house! Luckily, it serves at least eight people. It takes time to firm up, so make this dessert the night before you plan to enjoy a slice.

I can't tell you why it acquired the name "possum pie," but I do know it makes an easy, party-friendly dessert that can be made well in advance. To keep it a summer-friendly, no-cook recipe, use instant pudding with a little less milk than the box recipe suggests, so it firms up enough to be cleanly sliced. It's important to use a deep-dish pie plate, as the layers are thick.

1. Prepare Graham-Pecan Crust. Let chill in the refrigerator.

2. Beat ½ cup heavy cream in a mixing bowl with an electric mixer until soft peaks form. Transfer to another bowl. Beat cream cheese and ⅓ cup powdered sugar in the same mixing bowl (no need to wash bowl) until smooth. Fold in whipped cream. Spread mixture in bottom of chilled crust.

3. Whisk together pudding mix and cold milk in a bowl until smooth and slightly thickened. Spread pudding over cream cheese mixture.

4. Clean mixing bowl. Combine remaining ¾ cup heavy cream, remaining 1 tablespoon powdered sugar, and vanilla. Beat until soft peaks form. Spread or pipe over pudding layer.

5. Chill pie in the refrigerator for at least 4 hours or overnight. Garnish, if desired.

Graham-Pecan Crust: Combine **12 crushed graham crackers** in a food processor and process until fine crumbs form (1½ cups). Add **½ cup toasted, finely chopped pecan pieces** and pulse until uniformly blended. Add **6 tablespoons melted unsalted butter** and **2 tablespoons granulated sugar** and process until well blended. Press mixture firmly into bottom and up sides of a 9-inch deep-dish pie plate. Makes 1 piecrust.

CHOCOLATE-COVERED PECAN PIE BALLS

MAKES ABOUT 3 DOZEN

1 cup graham cracker crumbs
½ cup firmly packed light brown sugar
¼ cup maple syrup or honey
1 teaspoon vanilla extract
⅛ teaspoon fine sea salt
1¾ cups finely chopped toasted pecans
¼ cup melted salted or unsalted butter
6 ounces dark or semisweet chocolate, chopped
½ teaspoon coconut oil
Garnish: chopped pecans

These no-bake pecan pie balls capture all the warm, nutty flavors of a classic pecan pie in bite-size form—without the need for an oven. For an extra-indulgent touch, roll them in melted chocolate.

1. Combine graham crackers, brown sugar, maple syrup, vanilla, and salt in a food processor. Process until crackers are finely ground and mixture is well blended. Add pecans. Process until pecans are finely chopped. Add butter and process until mixture holds together when pressed into a ball.

2. Scoop mixture into 1-inch balls and place on a parchment paper-lined tray or baking sheet. Refrigerate for at least 30 minutes or until firm.

3. Combine chocolate and coconut oil in a small glass bowl; microwave in 30-second bursts, stirring each time. Roll each ball in chocolate mixture, letting excess chocolate drain, and place back on parchment. Garnish, if desired. Refrigerate for at least 30 minutes or until chocolate sets. Place in an airtight container and store in the refrigerator for up to 1 week.

NO-BAKE CHOCOLATE-TOPPED PEANUT BUTTER-OAT CUPS

MAKES 1 DOZEN

⅓ cup creamy peanut butter

¼ cup honey

1 teaspoon vanilla extract

¼ teaspoon fine sea salt

1½ cups quick oats (do not use old-fashioned oats)

6 ounces semisweet chocolate, chopped

⅓ cup whipping cream

Chopped peanuts

These no-bake cups combine chewy oats, creamy peanut butter, and rich chocolate for an easy, wholesome treat. Sweetened with honey, they're naturally delicious and require no oven time. Keep them in the fridge for a quick snack or dessert!

1. Heat peanut butter in a large microwave-safe bowl for 30 seconds or until very soft. Stir in honey, vanilla, and salt. Stir in oats.

2. Line a 12-cup muffin pan with paper liners. Divide oat mixture evenly among cups and press into bottom of paper liners.

3. Place chocolate and cream in a glass measuring cup or other microwave-safe container. Melt chocolate in 30-second intervals, stirring occasionally, until melted and smooth. Spread chocolate over oat mixture. Sprinkle with nuts.

4. Place in the freezer until firm. Store in an airtight container in the refrigerator for up to 1 week or freeze up to 3 months.

RAW PECAN-AND-DATE BROWNIES

MAKES ABOUT 1½ DOZEN

1½ cups Medjool dates, pitted (about 15 large dates)

1½ cups raw or toasted pecans

⅓ cup unsweetened cocoa powder

½ teaspoon espresso powder or finely ground instant coffee

1 teaspoon vanilla extract

¼ teaspoon fine sea salt

Cocoa-Almond Butter Frosting (recipe at right)

These flourless frosted brownies are served cold, bringing a refreshing burst of chocolate when temperatures are high.

These gluten-free, raw brownies are rich, chewy, and naturally sweetened with dates—no refined sugar needed! Pecans add a buttery texture, while cocoa and espresso powder give them a deep chocolate flavor. I prefer the richer taste of toasted pecans; I'll keep them in the freezer or buy toasted ones at stores like Trader Joe's. Serve these right out of the freezer. Although they're still delightful at room temperature, they will be soft and fudgy and may require a fork.

1. Line an 8x8-inch or 9x9-inch baking pan with parchment paper or nonstick aluminum foil. Combine dates and enough hot water to cover in a bowl. Let stand for 10 minutes or until dates soften; drain.

2. Place pecans in a food processor. Process until finely ground. Add dates, cocoa powder, espresso powder, vanilla, and salt. Process until well blended and mixture forms a sticky dough. Press mixture evenly into prepared baking pan. Freeze until firm.

3. Spread Cocoa-Almond Butter Frosting evenly over brownies. Cover and freeze until firm. Store in the freezer for up to 3 months.

Cocoa-Almond Butter Frosting: Beat **½ cup almond butter (no sugar added)** and **⅓ cup maple syrup** in a bowl with an electric mixer until light and fluffy. Slowly beat in **¼ cup cocoa powder, ½ teaspoon vanilla extract,** and **⅛ teaspoon fine sea salt.** Makes 1 cup.

EQUIVALENTS

Almonds	1 pound shelled	4 cups slivered	
Bacon	1 slice bacon	1 tablespoon crumbled	
Beans (Black)	1 pound dried	2⅓ cups uncooked	4¼ cups cooked
Beans (Black)	1 (15½-ounce) can	2 cups cooked	
Beans (Green)	1 pound fresh	3½ cups	
Beans (Green)	9 ounces frozen	1½ cups	
Beans (Green)	1 (15½-ounce) can	1¾ cups	
Bell Peppers	1 large	1 cup chopped	
Blueberries	1 pint fresh	2 cups	
Blueberries	10 ounces frozen	1½ cups	
Butter	1 stick	½ cup	8 tablespoons
Butter	2 sticks	1 cup	½ pound
Butter	4 sticks	2 cups	1 pound
Carrots	1 pound fresh	2½ cups grated	
Celery	2 medium ribs	½ cup chopped	
Cheese	4 ounces	1 cup shredded	
Cheese (Blue, Feta)	¼ pound	1 cup crumbled	
Cheese (Cheddar, Swiss, Jack)	8 ounces	2 cups shredded	
Cheese (Parmesan, Romano)	4 ounces	1 cup grated	
Corn	2 medium ears	1 cup kernels	
Crackers	28 soda or saltine crackers	1 cup crumbs	
Crackers	15 graham squares	1 cup crumbs	
Garlic	1 clove	½ teaspoon minced	
Lemon	1 medium	2 tablespoons juice	
Lemon	1 medium	2 teaspoons zest	
Lime	1 medium	1½ tablespoons juice	
Lime	1 medium	1 teaspoon zest	
Nuts	1 pound shelled	4 cups chopped	
Onion	1 large onion	1 cup chopped	

Orange	1 medium	⅓ cup juice	
Orange	1 medium	2 tablespoons zest	
Pasta	2 ounces uncooked	1 serving cooked	
Pasta	1 cup uncooked small macaroni	2 cups cooked	
Pasta	4 ounces uncooked spaghetti	4 cups cooked	
Rice	1 cup long-grain uncooked	3 cups cooked	
Sour Cream	8 ounces	1 cup	
Strawberries	1 pint	2 cups sliced	
Tomato	1 large	1 cup chopped	
Whipping Cream	1 cup	2 cups whipped	

MEASUREMENT CONVERSIONS

Pinch	less than ⅛ teaspoon
3 teaspoons	1 tablespoon
2 tablespoons	⅛ cup
4 tablespoons	¼ cup
5⅓ tablespoons	⅓ cup
8 tablespoons	½ cup
16 tablespoons	1 cup
1 tablespoon	½ fluid ounce
2 tablespoons	1 fluid ounce
¼ cup	2 fluid ounces
½ cup	4 fluid ounces
1 cup	8 fluid ounces
2 cups	16 fluid ounces
4 cups	32 fluid ounces
½ cup	¼ pint
1 cup	½ pint
2 cups	1 pint
4 cups	1 quart
4 quarts	1 gallon
16 cups	1 gallon

BAKING DISH CONVERSIONS

ROUND	
8x1½-inch	4 cups
8x2-inch	6 cups
9x1½-inch	6 cups
9x2-inch	8 cups
SQUARE	
8x8x1½-inch	6 cups
9x9x1½-inch	2 quarts
9x9x2-inch	2½ quarts
RECTANGLE	
11x7x2-inch	2½ quarts
13x9x2-inch	3 quarts
LOAF	
8½x4½x2½-inch	1½ quarts
9x5x3-inch	2 quarts
BUNDT—1 QUART	
9x3-inch	9 cups
10x3-inch	12 cups

SUBSTITUTIONS

BAKING POWDER	
1 teaspoon	¼ teaspoon baking soda + ½ teaspoon cream of tartar
BISCUIT MIX	
1 cup	1 cup all-purpose flour + 1½ teaspoons baking powder + 2 tablespoons shortening or butter
BREADCRUMBS	
1 cup	¾ cup cracker crumbs
BROTH	
1 cup	1 cup boiling water + 1 bouillon cube or 1 teaspoon granules or paste
BUTTERMILK	
1 cup	1 cup milk + 1 tablespoon lemon juice or vinegar
1 cup	1 cup plain yogurt
CHOCOLATE	
1 ounce unsweetened	3 tablespoons cocoa powder + 1 tablespoon butter or vegetable oil
1 ounce unsweetened	1½ ounces semisweet and remove 1 tablespoon sugar from recipe
1 ounce bittersweet or semisweet	⅔ ounce unsweetened chocolate + 2 teaspoons sugar
1 ounce bittersweet	1 ounce semisweet
1 ounce semisweet	1 ounce unsweetened + 1 tablespoon sugar
1 ounce sweet baking chocolate	3 tablespoons cocoa powder + 4 teaspoons sugar + 1 tablespoon butter or vegetable oil
CORN SYRUP (LIGHT)	
1 cup	¾ cup sugar + ¼ cup additional liquid in recipe
CORN SYRUP (DARK)	
1 cup	¾ cup light corn syrup + ¼ cup molasses
FLOUR, ALL-PURPOSE FLOUR (FOR THICKENING)	
2 tablespoons	1 tablespoon cornstarch
2 tablespoons	2 tablespoons quick-cooking tapioca
FLOUR, CAKE	
1 cup	1 cup - 2 tablespoons all-purpose flour + 2 tablespoons cornstarch

FLOUR, SELF-RISING	
1 cup	1 cup all-purpose flour + 1½ teaspoons baking powder + ⅛ teaspoon salt
HALF-AND-HALF	
1 cup	½ cup milk + ½ cup whipping cream
HERBS	
1 tablespoon fresh	1 teaspoon dried
LEMON JUICE	
1 teaspoon fresh juice	½ teaspoon vinegar
MOLASSES	
1 cup	1 cup almond butter
PEANUT BUTTER	
1 cup	1 cup almond butter
SUGAR (LIGHT BROWN)	
1 cup	½ cup dark brown sugar + ½ cup granulated sugar
SUGAR (GRANULATED)	
1 cup	1¾ cups powdered
1 cup	1 cup firmly packed light brown sugar
TOMATO SAUCE	
2 cups	1 cup tomato paste + 1 cup water

INDEX

A

All-the-Red-Things Chilled Soup, 82–83
almond butter
    Cocoa-Almond Butter Frosting, 172–173
    No-Bake Chocolate-Almond Breakfast Cookies, 56–57
almond-flavored liqueur
    Tiki Blush, 44
almond milk
    Brown Sugar-Cinnamon Overnight Oatmeal, 53
    Chocolate Brownie-Batter Hummus, 157
    Creamy Kale-and-Cashew Smoothie, 52
amaretto liqueur
    Tiki Blush, 44
    Whiskey Amaretto Slushie, 49
Antipasto Salad with Marinated Artichokes, Beans, Slivered Meats, and Creamy Hummus Dressing, 141
appetizers
    Beet-and-Goat Cheese Crostini, 25
    Chilled Shrimp with Two Sauces, 29
    Chipotle-Lime Guacamole, 15
    Cóctel de Camarones, 28
    Cranberry Salsa, 16
    Goat Cheese-and-Pistachio Grapes, 32
    Lemon-Ricotta Lima Bean Dip, 19
    Marinated Peppers with Capers and Basil, 23
    Muhammara, 20
    Peach-and-Blue Cheese Crostini with Balsamic Glaze, 24
    Pineapple Salsa, 18
    Quick, Fresh Heirloom Salsa, 14
    Roasted Red Pepper Hummus, 17
    Smoked Salmon Bruschetta with Arugula Pesto, 26
    Smoked Trout Dip, 35
    Smoky Cheddar-Pecan Cheese Ball, 27
    Smoky Chipotle-Bacon Deviled Eggs, 33
    Smoky Salmon Dip, 21
    Southern Pickled Shrimp, 36–37
    Sun-dried Tomato-and-Pesto Torta, 30–31
    Watermelon-Feta-Cucumber Bites with Balsamic Glaze, 22
    West Indies Crab Salad, 34

apples
    Chicken Waldorf Salad, 118
    Fall Greens with Smoked Trout, Pear, Cranberry, and Date Vinaigrette, 143
artichoke hearts
    Antipasto Salad with Marinated Artichokes, Beans, Slivered Meats, and Creamy Hummus Dressing, 141
arugula
    Arugula Pesto, 26
    Chicken, Orange, and Hazelnut Salad Bowl with Honey-Orange Dressing, 126
    Chicken, Prosciutto, and Goat Cheese Sandwiches, 67
    Chicken Salad Bowl with Five-Spice Vinaigrette, 130
    Elevated Cream Cheese-and-Olive Sandwiches, 62
    Fall Greens with Smoked Trout, Pear, Cranberry, and Date Vinaigrette, 143
    Greek Chicken-and-Zucchini Wrap, 69
    Hearty Cuban Salad with Mojo Vinaigrette, 140
    Open-faced Avocado-Egg Sandwich, 54
    Peach-and-Blue Cheese Crostini with Balsamic Glaze, 24
    Simple Beet-and-Arugula Salad with Whipped Ricotta and Honey Vinaigrette, 109
    Smoked Salmon-and-Beet Salad with Gribiche Dressing, 146
    Smoked Salmon Bruschetta with Arugula Pesto, 26
    Spicy Chicken-and-Mango Salad Bowl with Cilantro-Lime Vinaigrette, 128
    Turkey with Rosemary-Orange Marmalade Sauce, 64
Arugula Pesto, 26
Avocado-Ranch Dressing
    Chopped Salad with Avocado-Ranch Dressing, 104
avocados
    Avocado-Ranch Dressing, 104
    California Roll Bowl, 147
    Chicken-and-Grain Bowl with Creamy Green Goddess Dressing, 127
    Chilled Avocado Soup, 80
    Chipotle-Lime Guacamole, 15
    Chopped Salad with Avocado-Ranch Dressing, 104
    Hearts of Palm, Grapefruit, and Avocado Salad, 97
    Hearty Cuban Salad with Mojo Vinaigrette, 140
    Open-faced Avocado-Egg Sandwich, 54
    Tomato-and-Avocado Salad, 90

B

bacon
    Smoky Chipotle-Bacon Deviled Eggs, 33
Bahn Mi Sandwiches, 65
Balsamic Glaze
    Marinated Heirloom Tomatoes with Burrata, 89
balsamic vinegar
    Beet-and-Goat Cheese Crostini, 25
    Blue Cheese-Balsamic Vinaigrette, 137
    Peach-and-Blue Cheese Crostini with Balsamic Glaze, 24
    Watermelon-Feta-Cucumber Bites with Balsamic Glaze, 22
bananas
    Creamy Kale-and-Cashew Smoothie, 52
    No-Bake Banana Cream Pie with Chocolate Layer, 166
Basic Red Wine Vinaigrette
    Mediterranean Hummus Wrap with Vinaigrette, 68
basil
    Chilled Zucchini-and-Basil Soup, 84
    Creamy Green Goddess Dressing, 127
    Heirloom Tomato Panzanella with Brie and Basil, 100–101
    Herbed Buttermilk Dressing, 88
    Lemony Herbed Chicken Salad, 116
    Marinated Peppers with Capers and Basil, 23
    Tomato Salad with Herbed Buttermilk Dressing, 88
basil pesto
    Sun-dried Tomato-and-Pesto Torta, 30–31
basmati rice
    Greek Chicken Rice Bowl with Tzatziki Dressing, 132–133
beef
    Bahn Mi Sandwiches, 65

Beefsteak Salad with Blue Cheese-Balsamic Vinaigrette, 137
Roast Beef Salad with Heirloom Tomatoes and Thai Dressing, 138
Steak, Corn, and Tomato Salad with Smoky Cumin Vinaigrette, 136
Watercress-and-Roast Beef Salad with Chimichurri Vinaigrette, 139
Beefsteak Salad with Blue Cheese-Balsamic Vinaigrette, 137
Beet, Orange, and Blue Cheese Salad with Tarragon Vinaigrette, 108
Beet-and-Goat Cheese Crostini, 25
beets
    All-the-Red-Things Chilled Soup, 82
    Beet, Orange, and Blue Cheese Salad with Tarragon Vinaigrette, 108
    Beet-and-Goat Cheese Crostini, 25
    Simple Beet-and-Arugula Salad with Whipped Ricotta and Honey Vinaigrette, 109
    Smoked Salmon-and-Beet Salad with Gribiche Dressing, 146
bell peppers
    All-the-Red-Things Chilled Soup, 82–83
    Marinated Peppers with Capers and Basil, 23
    Muhammara, 20
    Roasted Red Pepper Hummus, 17
berries. *See also specific types*
    Brown Sugar-Cinnamon Overnight Oatmeal, 53
    No-Churn Mixed-Berry Ice Cream, 154
Berry-Cheesecake Cups, 162
beverages
    Bushwacker Shake, 47
    Creamy Kale-and-Cashew Smoothie, 52
    Frozen Gin and Tonic, 45
    Hibiscus Tea Lemonade, 40
    Limoncello Mojito, 48
    Mocha Punch, 46
    Tiki Blush, 44
    Tropical Sangría, 42
    Watermelon Agua Fresca, 41
    Whiskey Amaretto Slushie, 49
    White Linen Cocktail, 43
Bibb lettuce
    Bibb Salad with Raspberries, Mango, Hazelnuts, Goat Cheese, and Raspberry Vinaigrette, 107
    Crawfish Remoulade, 150–151
    Spicy Lentil Lettuce Wraps, 73
Bibb Salad with Raspberries, Mango, Hazelnuts, Goat Cheese, and Raspberry Vinaigrette, 107

black beans
    Chicken-and-Black Bean Tostadas, 74–75
blackberries
    Gingersnap-and-Berries Tart, 164
black-eyed peas
    Shrimp-and-Hoppin' John Salad, 149
    Southern Chicken, Tomato, and Black-eyed Pea Salad, 119
Blended Ginger Dressing
    Simple Side Salad with Blended Ginger Dressing, 105
blueberries
    Berry-Cheesecake Cups, 162
    Cantaloupe-and-Blueberry Salad with Honey, Lime, and Mint, 92
blue cheese
    Beet, Orange, and Blue Cheese Salad with Tarragon Vinaigrette, 108
    Blue Cheese-Balsamic Vinaigrette, 137
    Buttermilk-Blue Cheese Dressing, 91
    Easy Chicken Cobb Salad with Dijon Vinaigrette, 120–121
    Peach-and-Blue Cheese Crostini with Balsamic Glaze, 24
    Strawberry-Spinach Salad with Toasted Pecans and Honey-Poppy Seed Dressing, 103
Blue Cheese-Balsamic Vinaigrette
    Beefsteak Salad with Blue Cheese-Balsamic Vinaigrette, 137
breakfast
    Brown Sugar-Cinnamon Overnight Oatmeal, 53
    Creamy Kale-and-Cashew Smoothie, 52
    No-Bake Chocolate-Almond Breakfast Cookies, 56–57
    Open-Faced Avocado-Egg Salad Sandwich, 54
    Smoked Salmon Breakfast Wrap, 55
Brown Sugar-Cinnamon Overnight Oatmeal, 53
bulgur wheat
    Moroccan Kale-and-Grain Salad With Cumin-Coriander Vinaigrette, 102
    Za'Atar Chicken, Bulgur, and Lentil Salad Bowl, 134
burrata cheese
    Marinated Heirloom Tomatoes with Burrata, 89
Bushwacker Shake, 47
buttermilk
    Avocado-Ranch Dressing, 104
    Buttermilk-Blue Cheese Dressing, 91
    Herbed Buttermilk Dressing, 88

Buttermilk-Blue Cheese Dressing
    Wedge Salad with Buttermilk-Blue Cheese Dressing, 91

C

cabbage
    Chicken-and-Napa Cabbage Salad with Sesame-Soy Vinaigrette, 125
    Kale Salad with Orange-Sesame Dressing, 106
    Salad Bowl with Curried Miso Dressing, 135
    Simple Side Salad with Blended Ginger Dressing, 105
    Tex-Mex Coleslaw with Creamy Lime-Chipotle Dressing, 111
California Roll Bowl, 147
cannellini beans
    Antipasto Salad with Marinated Artichokes, Beans, Slivered Meats, and Creamy Hummus Dressing, 141
    Mediterranean White Bean Salad, 99
Cantaloupe-and-Blueberry Salad with Honey, Lime, and Mint, 92
capers
    Caper-Shallot Vinaigrette, 142
    Marinated Peppers with Capers and Basil, 23
Caper-Shallot Vinaigrette
    Tuna Niçoise Salad with Caper-Shallot Vinaigrette, 142
Carrot, Mango, and Jicama Slaw, 110
carrots
    Carrot, Mango, and Jicama Slaw, 110
cashews
    Creamy Kale-and-Cashew Smoothie, 52
Cauliflower Chickpea Salad Bowl with Curry-Tahini Dressing, 96
celery
    Celery Salad with Dates, Walnuts, and Parmesan, 94
    Marinated Celery-and-Chickpea Salad with Lemon-Shallot Vinaigrette, 95
Celery Salad with Dates, Walnuts, and Parmesan, 94
cellophane noodles
    Veggie Summer Rolls with Hoisin Peanut Sauce, 72
cheddar cheese
    Pimiento Cheese, 61
    Smoky Cheddar-Pecan Cheese Ball, 27
cheese, 7, 11, 174. *See also specific types*

chicken
- Chicken, Orange, and Hazelnut Salad Bowl with Honey-Orange Dressing, 126
- Chicken, Prosciutto, and Goat Cheese Sandwiches, 67
- Chicken-and-Black Bean Tostadas, 74
- Chicken-and-Grain Bowl With Creamy Green Goddess Dressing, 127
- Chicken-and-Napa Cabbage Salad with Sesame-Soy Vinaigrette, 125
- Chicken Burrito Bowl with Creamy Chipotle Dressing, 131
- Chicken Caesar Salad with Chipotle Dressing, 123
- Chicken Noodle Bowl with Peanut-Coconut Dressing, 129
- Chicken Salad Bowl with Five-Spice Vinaigrette, 130
- Chicken Waldorf Salad, 118
- Crispy Fried Chicken Salad with Honey-Mustard Dressing, 124
- Easy Chicken Cobb Salad with Dijon Vinaigrette, 120–121
- Greek Chicken-and-Zucchini Wrap, 69
- Greek Chicken Rice Bowl with Tzatziki Dressing, 132–133
- Hearty Cuban Salad with Mojo Vinaigrette, 140
- Lemony Herbed Chicken Salad, 116
- Mexican Chicken Cobb Salad with Chipotle Ranch Dressing, 122
- No-Cook Chicken Salad Wraps, 70
- Quick Curried Chicken Salad, 117
- Salad Bowl with Curried Miso Dressing, 135
- Southern Chicken, Tomato, and Black-eyed Pea Salad, 119
- Spicy Chicken-and-Mango Salad Bowl with Cilantro-Lime Vinaigrette, 128
- Za'Atar Chicken, Bulgur, and Lentil Salad Bowl, 134

Chicken, Orange, and Hazelnut Salad Bowl with Honey-Orange Dressing, 126
Chicken, Prosciutto, and Goat Cheese Sandwiches, 67
Chicken-and-Black Bean Tostadas, 74
Chicken-and-Grain Bowl with Creamy Green Goddess Dressing, 127
Chicken-and-Napa Cabbage Salad with Sesame-Soy Vinaigrette, 125
Chicken Burrito Bowl with Creamy Chipotle Dressing, 131
Chicken Caesar Salad with Chipotle Dressing, 123
Chicken Noodle Bowl with Peanut-Coconut Dressing, 129

Chicken Waldorf Salad, 118
chickpeas
- Antipasto Salad with Marinated Artichokes, Beans, Slivered Meats, and Creamy Hummus Dressing, 141
- Cauliflower Chickpea Salad Bowl with Curry-Tahini Dressing, 96
- Marinated Celery-and-Chickpea Salad with Lemon-Shallot Vinaigrette, 95

chili sauce
- Chilled Shrimp with Two Sauces, 29
- Quick Cocktail Sauce, 29

Chilled Avocado Soup, 80
Chilled Cucumber Soup, 79
Chilled Shrimp with Two Sauces, 29
Chilled Zucchini-and-Basil Soup, 84
Chimichurri Vinaigrette
- Watercress-and-Roast Beef Salad with Chimichurri Vinaigrette, 139

Chipotle Dressing
- Chicken Caesar Salad with Chipotle Dressing, 123

Chipotle-Lime Guacamole, 15
chipotle peppers
- Chipotle Dressing, 123
- Chipotle-Lime Guacamole, 15
- Chipotle Ranch Dressing, 122
- Creamy Chipotle Dressing, 131
- Smoky Chipotle-Bacon Deviled Eggs, 33
- Tex-Mex Coleslaw with Creamy Lime-Chipotle Dressing, 111

Chipotle Ranch Dressing
- Mexican Chicken Cobb Salad with Chipotle Ranch Dressing, 122

chocolate
- Chocolate-Covered Pecan Pie Balls, 170
- Chocolate Ganache, 167
- No-Bake Banana Cream Pie with Chocolate Layer, 166
- No-Bake Chocolate-Almond Breakfast Cookies, 56–57
- No-Bake Chocolate Cheesecake with Chocolate Cookie Crust, 163
- No-Bake Chocolate-Topped Peanut Butter-Oat Cups, 171
- Tiramisu, 158

Chocolate Brownie-Batter Hummus, 157
chocolate cookie crust
- Frozen Peanut Butter Pie, 167
Chocolate-Covered Pecan Pie Balls, 170
Chocolate Ganache
- Frozen Peanut Butter Pie, 167

Chocolate-Hazelnut Ice Cream, 156
chocolate ice cream
- Mocha Punch, 46
chocolate pudding mix
- Possum Pie, 168–169
chocolate sandwich cookies
- No-Bake Chocolate Cheesecake With Chocolate Cookie Crust, 163
Chopped Salad with Avocado-Ranch Dressing, 104
Cilantro-Lime Vinaigrette
- Spicy Chicken-and-Mango Salad Bowl With Cilantro-Lime Vinaigrette, 128
cinnamon
- Brown Sugar-Cinnamon Overnight Oatmeal, 53
Cocoa-Almond Butter Frosting
- Raw Pecan-and-Date Brownies, 172–173
cocoa powder
- Chocolate Brownie-Batter Hummus, 157
- Cocoa-Almond Butter Frosting, 172–173
- Mocha Punch, 46
- No-Bake Chocolate-Almond Breakfast Cookies, 56–57
- Raw Pecan-and-Date Brownies, 172–173
coconut cream
- Bushwacker Shake, 47
- No-Bake Chocolate-Almond Breakfast Cookies, 56–57
coconut milk
- Peanut-Coconut Dressing, 129
Cóctel de Camarones, 28
coffee
- Mocha Punch, 46
- Raw Pecan-and-Date Brownies, 172
- Tiramisu, 158
coffee liqueur
- Bushwacker Shake, 47
- Tiramisu, 158
Colby-Jack cheese
- Crispy Fried Chicken Salad with Honey-Mustard Dressing, 124
couscous
- Couscous-Tabbouleh Salad, 98
- Moroccan Kale-and-Grain Salad with Cumin-Coriander Vinaigrette, 102
Couscous-Tabbouleh Salad, 98
crabmeat
- California Roll Bowl, 147
- West Indies Crab Salad, 34

cranberries
  Cranberry Salsa, 16
  Fall Greens with Smoked Trout, Pear, Cranberry, and Date Vinaigrette, 143
Cranberry Salsa, 16
Crawfish Rémoulade, 150–151
cream cheese
  Berry-Cheesecake Cups, 162
  Elevated Cream Cheese-and-Olive Sandwiches, 62
  Frozen Peanut Butter Pie, 167
  Gingersnap-and-Berries Tart, 164
  Lemon Icebox Pie, 165
  No-Bake Chocolate Cheesecake with Chocolate Cookie Crust, 163
  Pimiento Cheese, 61
  Possum Pie, 168–169
  Raspberry-and-Lemon Icebox Cake, 160–161
  Smoked Salmon Breakfast Wrap, 55
  Smoked Trout Dip, 35
  Smoky Cheddar-Pecan Cheese Ball, 27
  Smoky Salmon Dip, 21
  Sun-dried Tomato-and-Pesto Torta, 30–31
Creamy Chipotle Dressing
  Chicken Burrito Bowl with Creamy Chipotle Dressing, 131
Creamy Cucumber-and-Sweet Onion Salad, 93
Creamy Green Goddess Dressing
  Chicken-and-Grain Bowl with Creamy Green Goddess Dressing, 127
Creamy Hummus Dressing
  Antipasto Salad with Marinated Artichokes, Beans, Slivered Meats, and Creamy Hummus Dressing, 141
Creamy Kale-and-Cashew Smoothie, 52
Crispy Fried Chicken Salad with Honey-Mustard Dressing, 124
crostini
  Beet-and-Goat Cheese Crostini, 25
  Peach-and-Blue Cheese Crostini with Balsamic Glaze, 24
  Smoked Salmon Bruschetta with Arugula Pesto, 26
cucumbers
  California Roll Bowl, 147
  Chicken-and-Grain Bowl with Creamy Green Goddess Dressing, 127
  Chilled Cucumber Soup, 79
  Creamy Cucumber-and-Sweet Onion Salad, 93

  Frozen Gin and Tonic, 45
  Tzatziki Dressing, 132–133
  Watermelon-Feta-Cucumber Bites with Balsamic Glaze, 22
  White Gazpacho With Cucumber, 85
  White Linen Cocktail, 43
cumin
  Cumin-Coriander Vinaigrette, 102
  Smoky Cumin Vinaigrette, 136
Cumin-Coriander Vinaigrette
  Moroccan Kale-and-Grain Salad with Cumin-Coriander Vinaigrette, 102
Curried Miso Dressing
  Salad Bowl with Curried Miso Dressing, 135
curry powder
  Curried Miso Dressing, 135
  Curry-Tahini Dressing, 96
  Quick Curried Chicken Salad, 117
Curry-Tahini Dressing
  Cauliflower Chickpea Salad Bowl with Curry-Tahini Dressing, 96

D

dates
  Celery Salad with Dates, Walnuts, and Parmesan, 94
  Date Vinaigrette, 143
  Gingersnap-Date Crust, 164
  Raw Pecan-and-Date Brownies, 172
Date Vinaigrette
  Fall Greens with Smoked Trout, Pear, Cranberry, and Date Vinaigrette, 143
desserts
  Berry-Cheesecake Cups, 162
  Chocolate Brownie-Batter Hummus, 157
  Chocolate-Covered Pecan Pie Balls, 170
  Chocolate-Hazelnut Ice Cream, 156
  Frozen Peanut Butter Pie, 167
  Gingersnap-and-Berries Tart, 164
  Lemon Icebox Pie, 165
  No-Bake Banana Cream Pie with Chocolate Layer, 166
  No-Bake Chocolate-Almond Breakfast Cookies, 56–57
  No-Bake Chocolate Cheesecake with Chocolate Cookie Crust, 163
  No-Bake Chocolate-Topped Peanut Butter-Oat Cups, 171
  No-Churn Mixed-Berry Ice Cream, 154
  Possum Pie, 168–169
  Raspberry-and-Lemon Icebox Cake, 160–161

  Raw Pecan-and-Date Brownies, 172
  Strawberry Brownie Trifle Cups, 159
  Super Quick-and-Easy Peach Sherbet, 155
  Tiramisu, 158
Dijon mustard
  Dijon Vinaigrette, 120–121
  Honey-Mustard Dressing, 124
Dijon Vinaigrette
  Easy Chicken Cobb Salad with Dijon Vinaigrette, 120–121
dill
  Dilled Egg Salad, 60
  Tzatziki Dressing, 132–133
Dilled Egg Salad, 60
dill pickles
  Ham Salad, 63
  Smoky Chipotle-Bacon Deviled Eggs, 33
dressings. *See* sauces and dressings
drinks. *See* beverages
Dynamite Sauce
  California Roll Bowl, 147

E

Easy Chicken Cobb Salad with Dijon Vinaigrette, 120–121
eggs
  Dilled Egg Salad, 60
  Easy Chicken Cobb Salad with Dijon Vinaigrette, 120–121
  Mexican Chicken Cobb Salad with Chipotle Ranch Dressing, 122
  Open-faced Avocado-Egg Sandwich, 54
  Smoky Chipotle-Bacon Deviled Eggs, 33
  Tuna Niçoise Salad with Caper-Shallot Vinaigrette, 142
Elevated Cream Cheese-and-Olive Sandwiches, 62
espresso
  Raw Pecan-and-Date Brownies, 172
  Tiramisu, 158

F

Fall Greens with Smoked Trout, Pear, Cranberry, and Date Vinaigrette, 143
farro
  Chicken-and-Grain Bowl with Creamy Green Goddess Dressing, 127
  Moroccan Kale-and-Grain Salad with Cumin-Coriander Vinaigrette, 102
  Za'Atar Chicken, Bulgur, and Lentil Salad Bowl, 134

feta cheese
    Watermelon-Feta-Cucumber Bites with Balsamic Glaze, 22

fish and seafood
    Chilled Shrimp with Two Sauces, 29
    Cóctel de Camarones, 28
    Crawfish Rémoulade, 150–151
    Fall Greens with Smoked Trout, Pear, Cranberry, and Date Vinaigrette, 143
    Lemony Lobster Rolls, 66
    Quinoa-and-Smoked Salmon Kale Bowl with Lemon-Tahini Dressing, 145
    Shrimp-and-Glass Noodle Salad, 148
    Shrimp-and-Hoppin' John Salad, 149
    Smoked Salmon-and-Beet Salad with Gribiche Dressing, 146
    Smoked Salmon Breakfast Wrap, 55
    Smoked Salmon Bruschetta with Arugula Pesto, 26
    Smoked Sockeye Caesar Salad with Lemony Dressing, 144
    Smoked Trout Dip, 35
    Smoky Salmon Dip, 21
    Southern Pickled Shrimp, 36–37
    West Indies Crab Salad, 34

Five-Spice Vinaigrette
    Chicken Salad Bowl with Five-Spice Vinaigrette, 130

Frozen Gin and Tonic, 45

Frozen Peanut Butter Pie, 167

G

gin
    White Linen Cocktail, 43

ginger ale
    Blended Ginger Dressing, 105
    Creamy Kale-and-Cashew Smoothie, 52
    Whiskey Amaretto Slushie, 49

Gingersnap-and-Berries Tart, 164

gingersnap cookies
    Gingersnap-Date Crust, 164

Gingersnap-Date Crust
    Gingersnap-and-Berries Tart, 164

goat cheese
    Beet-and-Goat Cheese Crostini, 25
    Bibb Salad with Raspberries, Mango, Hazelnuts, Goat Cheese, and Raspberry Vinaigrette, 107
    Chicken, Prosciutto, and Goat Cheese Sandwiches, 67
    Goat Cheese-and-Pistachio Grapes, 32

Goat Cheese-and-Pistachio Grapes, 32

Golden Tomato-and-Peach Gazpacho, 81

Graham Cracker Crust
    Frozen Peanut Butter Pie, 167
    Lemon Icebox Pie, 165
    No-Bake Banana Cream Pie with Chocolate Layer, 166

graham crackers
    Chocolate-Covered Pecan Pie Balls, 170
    Graham Cracker Crust, 165
    Graham-Pecan Crust, 168–169
    Raspberry-and-Lemon Icebox Cake, 160–161

Graham-Pecan Crust
    Possum Pie, 168–169

grains, 3, 8, 9. *See also specific types*

granola
    Berry-Cheesecake Cups, 162

grapefruit
    Hearts of Palm, Grapefruit, and Avocado Salad, 97

grapes
    Chicken Waldorf Salad, 118
    Goat Cheese-and-Pistachio Grapes, 32
    White Gazpacho with Cucumber, 85

Greek Chicken-and-Zucchini Wrap, 69

Greek Chicken Rice Bowl with Tzatziki Dressing, 132–133

green beans
    Tuna Niçoise Salad with Caper-Shallot Vinaigrette, 142

green lentils
    Za'Atar Chicken, Bulgur, and Lentil Salad Bowl, 134

Gribiche Dressing
    Smoked Salmon-and-Beet Salad with Gribiche Dressing, 146

H

Ham Salad, 63

hard-boiled eggs, 6, 9

hazelnuts
    Bibb Salad with Raspberries, Mango, Hazelnuts, Goat Cheese, and Raspberry Vinaigrette, 107
    Chicken, Orange, and Hazelnut Salad Bowl with Honey-Orange Dressing, 126

Hearts of Palm, Grapefruit, and Avocado Salad, 97

Hearty Cuban Salad with Mojo Vinaigrette, 140

heavy cream
    Chocolate Ganache, 167
    Chocolate-Hazelnut Ice Cream, 156
    Mocha Punch, 46
    No-Churn Mixed-Berry Ice Cream, 154
    Strawberry-Brownie Trifle Cups, 159
    Tiramisu, 158

Heirloom Tomato Panzanella with Brie and Basil, 100–101

Herbed Buttermilk Dressing
    Tomato Salad with Herbed Buttermilk Dressing, 88

Hibiscus Tea Lemonade, 40

Hoisin-Peanut Dipping Sauce
    Veggie Summer Rolls with Hoisin Peanut Sauce, 72

hoisin sauce
    Hoisin-Peanut Dipping Sauce, 72

honey
    Cantaloupe-and-Blueberry Salad with Honey, Lime, and Mint, 92
    Honey-Mustard Dressing, 124
    Honey-Orange Dressing, 126
    Honey-Poppy Seed Dressing, 103
    Honey Vinaigrette, 109
    Simple Beet-and-Arugula Salad with Whipped Ricotta and Honey Vinaigrette, 109

Honey-Mustard Dressing
    Crispy Fried Chicken Salad with Honey-Mustard Dressing, 124

Honey-Orange Dressing
    Chicken, Orange, and Hazelnut Salad Bowl with Honey-Orange Dressing, 126

Honey-Poppy Seed Dressing
    Strawberry-Spinach Salad with Toasted Pecans and Honey-Poppy Seed Dressing, 103

Honey Vinaigrette
    Simple Beet-and-Arugula Salad with Whipped Ricotta and Honey Vinaigrette, 109

hummus
    Creamy Hummus Dressing, 141
    Mediterranean Hummus Wrap with Vinaigrette, 68

I

imitation crab
    California Roll Bowl, 147

J

jasmine rice
    Greek Chicken Rice Bowl with Tzatziki Dressing, 132–133

jicama
    Bahn Mi Sandwiches, 65
    Carrot, Mango, and Jicama Slaw, 110

K

kale
- Creamy Kale-and-Cashew Smoothie, 52
- Kale Salad with Orange-Sesame Dressing, 106
- Moroccan Kale-and-Grain Salad with Cumin-Coriander Vinaigrette, 102
- Quinoa-and-Smoked Salmon Kale Bowl with Lemon-Tahini Dressing, 145

Kale Salad with Orange-Sesame Dressing, 106

L

ladyfingers
- Tiramisu, 158

lemon curd
- Raspberry-and-Lemon Icebox Cake, 160–161
- Lemon Icebox Pie, 165
- Lemon-Ricotta Lima Bean Dip, 19

lemons
- Hibiscus Tea Lemonade, 40
- Lemon Icebox Pie, 165
- Lemon-Ricotta Lima Bean Dip, 19
- Lemon-Shallot Vinaigrette, 95
- Lemon-Tahini Dressing, 145
- Lemony Dressing, 144
- Lemony Herbed Chicken Salad, 116
- Lemony Lobster Rolls, 66
- Limoncello Mojito, 48

Lemon-Shallot Vinaigrette
- Marinated Celery-and-Chickpea Salad with Lemon-Shallot Vinaigrette, 95

Lemon-Tahini Dressing
- Quinoa-and-Smoked Salmon Kale Bowl with Lemon-Tahini Dressing, 145
- Za'Atar Chicken, Bulgur, and Lentil Salad Bowl, 134

Lemony Dressing
- Smoked Sockeye Caesar Salad with Lemony Dressing, 144

Lemony Herbed Chicken Salad, 116
Lemony Lobster Rolls, 66

lentils
- Spicy Lentil Lettuce Wraps, 73
- Za'Atar Chicken, Bulgur, and Lentil Salad Bowl, 134

lettuce
- Antipasto Salad with Marinated Artichokes, Beans, Slivered Meats, and Creamy Hummus Dressing, 141
- Beefsteak Salad with Blue Cheese-Balsamic Vinaigrette, 137
- Beet, Orange, and Blue Cheese Salad with Tarragon Vinaigrette, 108
- Bibb Salad with Raspberries, Mango, Hazelnuts, Goat Cheese, and Raspberry Vinaigrette, 107
- Chicken, Orange, and Hazelnut Salad Bowl with Honey-Orange Dressing, 126
- Chicken-and-Grain Bowl with Creamy Green Goddess Dressing, 127
- Chicken Burrito Bowl with Creamy Chipotle Dressing, 131
- Chicken Caesar Salad with Chipotle Dressing, 123
- Chicken Salad Bowl with Five-Spice Vinaigrette, 130
- Chopped Salad With Avocado-Ranch Dressing, 104
- Crawfish Rémoulade, 150–151
- Crispy Fried Chicken Salad with Honey-Mustard Dressing, 124
- Easy Chicken Cobb Salad with Dijon Vinaigrette, 120–121
- Fall Greens with Smoked Trout, Pear, Cranberry, and Date Vinaigrette, 143
- Greek Chicken Rice Bowl with Tzatziki Dressing, 132–133
- Hearty Cuban Salad with Mojo Vinaigrette, 140
- Mediterranean Hummus Wrap with Vinaigrette, 68
- Mexican Chicken Cobb Salad with Chipotle Ranch Dressing, 122
- No-Cook Chicken Salad Wraps, 70
- Roast Beef Salad with Heirloom Tomatoes and Thai Dressing, 138
- Salad Bowl with Curried Miso Dressing, 135
- Simple Side Salad with Blended Ginger Dressing, 105
- Smoked Salmon-and-Beet Salad with Gribiche Dressing, 146
- Smoked Sockeye Caesar Salad with Lemony Dressing, 144
- Southern Chicken, Tomato, and Black-eyed Pea Salad, 119
- Spicy Chicken-and-Mango Salad Bowl with Cilantro-Lime Vinaigrette, 128
- Spicy Lentil Lettuce Wraps, 73
- Steak, Corn, and Tomato Salad with Smoky Cumin Vinaigrette, 136
- Tuna Niçoise Salad with Caper-Shallot Vinaigrette, 142
- Veggie Summer Rolls with Hoisin Peanut Sauce, 72
- Wedge Salad with Buttermilk-Blue Cheese Dressing, 91

lima beans
- Lemon-Ricotta Lima Bean Dip, 19

limes
- Cantaloupe-and-Blueberry Salad with Honey, Lime, and Mint, 92
- Chipotle-Lime Guacamole, 15
- Cilantro-Lime Vinaigrette, 128
- Five-Spice Vinaigrette, 130
- Tex-Mex Coleslaw with Creamy Lime-Chipotle Dressing, 111

Limoncello Mojito, 48

lobster
- Lemony Lobster Rolls, 66

M

main-dish salads and bowls.
- Antipasto Salad with Marinated Artichokes, Beans, Slivered Meats, and Creamy Hummus Dressing, 141
- Beefsteak Salad with Blue Cheese-Balsamic Vinaigrette, 137
- California Roll Bowl, 147
- Chicken, Orange, and Hazelnut Salad Bowl with Honey-Orange Dressing, 126
- Chicken-and-Grain Bowl with Creamy Green Goddess Dressing, 127
- Chicken-and-Napa Cabbage Salad with Sesame-Soy Vinaigrette, 125
- Chicken Burrito Bowl with Creamy Chipotle Dressing, 131
- Chicken Caesar Salad with Chipotle Dressing, 123
- Chicken Noodle Bowl with Peanut-Coconut Dressing, 129
- Chicken Waldorf Salad, 118
- Crawfish Remoulade, 150–151
- Crispy Fried Chicken Salad with Honey-Mustard Dressing, 124
- Easy Chicken Cobb Salad with Dijon Vinaigrette, 120–121
- Fall Greens with Smoked Trout, Pear, Cranberry, and Date Vinaigrette, 143
- Chicken Salad Bowl with Five-Spice Vinaigrette, 130
- Greek Chicken Rice Bowl with Tzatziki Dressing, 132–133
- Hearty Cuban Salad with Mojo Vinaigrette, 140
- Lemony Herbed Chicken Salad, 116
- Mexican Chicken Cobb Salad with Chipotle Ranch Dressing, 122
- Quick Curried Chicken Salad, 117

Quinoa-and-Smoked Salmon Kale Bowl with Lemon-Tahini Dressing, 145
Roast Beef Salad with Heirloom Tomatoes and Thai Dressing, 138
Salad Bowl with Curried Miso Dressing, 135
Shrimp-and-Glass Noodle Salad, 148
Shrimp-and-Hoppin' John Salad, 149
Smoked Salmon-and-Beet Salad with Gribiche Dressing, 146
Smoked Sockeye Caesar Salad with Lemony Dressing, 144
Southern Chicken, Tomato, and Black-eyed Pea Salad, 119
Spicy Chicken-and-Mango Salad Bowl with Cilantro-Lime Vinaigrette, 128
Steak, Corn, and Tomato Salad with Smoky Cumin Vinaigrette, 136
Tuna Niçoise Salad with Caper-Shallot Vinaigrette, 142
Watercress-and-Roast Beef Salad with Chimichurri Vinaigrette, 139
Za'atar Chicken, Bulgur, and Lentil Salad Bowl, 134

mangoes
Bibb Salad with Raspberries, Mango, Hazelnuts, Goat Cheese, and Raspberry Vinaigrette, 107
Carrot, Mango, and Jicama Slaw, 110
Spicy Chicken-and-Mango Salad Bowl with Cilantro-Lime Vinaigrette, 128
Tropical Sangría, 42

Marinated Celery-and-Chickpea Salad with Lemon-Shallot Vinaigrette, 95
Marinated Heirloom Tomatoes with Burrata, 89
Marinated Peppers with Capers and Basil, 23

mascarpone cheese
Tiramisu, 158

Mediterranean Hummus Wrap with Vinaigrette, 68
Mediterranean White Bean Salad, 99

Medjool dates
Celery Salad with Dates, Walnuts, and Parmesan, 94
Creamy Kale-and-Cashew Smoothie, 52
Raw Pecan-and-Date Brownies, 172

Mexican Chicken Cobb Salad with Chipotle Ranch Dressing, 122

mint
Cantaloupe-and-Blueberry Salad with Honey, Lime, And Mint, 92
Limoncello Mojito, 48

miso paste
Curried Miso Dressing, 135
Mocha Punch, 46
Mojo Vinaigrette
Hearty Cuban Salad with Mojo Vinaigrette, 140
Moroccan Kale-and-Grain Salad with Cumin-Coriander Vinaigrette, 102
Muhammara, 20

N
Napa cabbage
Chicken-and-Napa Cabbage Salad with Sesame-Soy Vinaigrette, 125
No-Bake Banana Cream Pie with Chocolate Layer, 166
No-Bake Chocolate-Almond Breakfast Cookies, 56–57
No-Bake Chocolate Cheesecake with Chocolate Cookie Crust, 163
No-Bake Chocolate-Topped Peanut Butter-Oat Cups, 171
No-Churn Mixed-Berry Ice Cream, 154
No-Cook Chicken [Larb] Salad Wraps, 70–71
Nutella
Chocolate-Hazelnut Ice Cream, 156

O
oats
Brown Sugar-Cinnamon Overnight Oatmeal, 53
No-Bake Chocolate-Almond Breakfast Cookies, 56–57
No-Bake Chocolate-Topped Peanut Butter-Oat Cups, 171
olives
Elevated Cream Cheese-and-Olive Sandwiches, 62
onions, 10, 174
Open-faced Avocado-Egg Sandwich, 54
orange marmalade
Turkey with Rosemary-Orange Marmalade Sauce, 64
oranges
Beet, Orange, and Blue Cheese Salad with Tarragon Vinaigrette, 108
Chicken, Orange, and Hazelnut Salad Bowl with Honey-Orange Dressing, 126
Honey-Orange Dressing, 126
Orange-Sesame Dressing, 106
Tropical Sangría, 42
Orange-Sesame Dressing
Kale Salad with Orange-Sesame Dressing, 106

P
Parmesan cheese
Celery Salad with Dates, Walnuts, and Parmesan, 94
parsley
Chimichurri Vinaigrette, 139
Creamy Green Goddess Dressing, 127
Tomato Salad with Herbed Buttermilk Dressing, 88
Peach-and-Blue Cheese Crostini with Balsamic Glaze, 24
peaches
Golden Tomato-and-Peach Gazpacho, 81
Peach-and-Blue Cheese Crostini with Balsamic Glaze, 24
Super Quick-and-Easy Peach Sherbet, 155
Peanut-Coconut Dressing
Chicken Noodle Bowl with Peanut-Coconut Dressing, 129
peanuts/peanut butter
Frozen Peanut Butter Pie, 167
Hoisin-Peanut Dipping Sauce, 72
No-Bake Chocolate-Topped Peanut Butter-Oat Cups, 171
No-Cook Chicken Salad Wraps, 70
Peanut-Coconut Dressing, 129
Roast Beef Salad with Heirloom Tomatoes and Thai Dressing, 138
pears
Fall Greens with Smoked Trout, Pear, Cranberry, and Date Vinaigrette, 143
pecan crust
Frozen Peanut Butter Pie, 167
pecans
Chocolate-Covered Pecan Pie Balls, 170
Graham-Pecan Crust, 168–169
Raw Pecan-and-Date Brownies, 172
Smoky Cheddar-Pecan Cheese Ball, 27
Strawberry-Spinach Salad with Toasted Pecans and Honey-Poppy Seed Dressing, 103
pesto
Chicken, Prosciutto, and Goat Cheese Sandwiches, 67
Pimiento Cheese, 61
Pineapple Salsa, 18
pine nuts
Arugula Pesto, 26
Smoked Salmon Bruschetta with Arugula Pesto, 26
Sun-dried Tomato-and-Pesto Torta, 30

Za'Atar Chicken, Bulgur, and Lentil Salad Bowl, 134
pistachios
   Goat Cheese-and-Pistachio Grapes, 32
poppy seeds
   Honey-Poppy Seed Dressing, 103
Possum Pie, 168–169
prosciutto
   Antipasto Salad with Marinated Artichokes, Beans, Slivered Meats, and Creamy Hummus Dressing, 141
   Chicken, Prosciutto, and Goat Cheese Sandwiches, 67
provolone cheese
   Antipasto Salad with Marinated Artichokes, Beans, Slivered Meats, And Creamy Hummus Dressing, 141
   Simple Side Salad with Blended Ginger Dressing, 105

Q

Quick, Fresh Heirloom Salsa, 14
Quick Cocktail Sauce
   Chilled Shrimp with Two Sauces, 29
Quick Curried Chicken Salad, 117
quinoa
   Chicken-and-Grain Bowl with Creamy Green Goddess Dressing, 127
   Moroccan Kale-and-Grain Salad With Cumin-Coriander Vinaigrette, 102
   Quinoa-and-Smoked Salmon Kale Bowl with Lemon-Tahini Dressing, 145
   Salad Bowl with Curried Miso Dressing, 135
   Spicy Chicken-and-Mango Salad Bowl with Cilantro-Lime Vinaigrette, 128
   Za'Atar Chicken, Bulgur, and Lentil Salad Bowl, 134
Quinoa-and-Smoked Salmon Kale Bowl with Lemon-Tahini Dressing, 145

R

radishes
   Bahn Mi Sandwiches, 65
   Chicken Salad Bowl with Five-Spice Vinaigrette, 130
Ramen Noodle Slaw, 112–113
raspberries
   Bibb Salad with Raspberries, Mango, Hazelnuts, Goat Cheese, and Raspberry Vinaigrette, 107
   Gingersnap-and-Berries Tart, 164
   Raspberry-and-Lemon Icebox Cake, 160–161
   Raspberry Vinaigrette, 107
   Tropical Sangría, 42
Raspberry-and-Lemon Icebox Cake, 160–161
raspberry lemonade
   Tiki Blush, 44
raspberry preserves
   Raspberry-and-Lemon Icebox Cake, 160–161
Raspberry Vinaigrette
   Bibb Salad with Raspberries, Mango, Hazelnuts, Goat Cheese, and Raspberry Vinaigrette, 107
Raw Pecan-and-Date Brownies, 172
red cabbage
   Chicken-and-Napa Cabbage Salad with Sesame-Soy Vinaigrette, 125
   Salad Bowl with Curried Miso Dressing, 135
rice
   California Roll Bowl, 147
   Chicken-and-Grain Bowl With Creamy Green Goddess Dressing, 127
   Chicken Burrito Bowl with Creamy Chipotle Dressing, 131
   Greek Chicken Rice Bowl with Tzatziki Dressing, 132–133
   Salad Bowl With Curried Miso Dressing, 135
   Shrimp-and-Hoppin' John Salad, 149
rice noodles
   Chicken Noodle Bowl with Peanut-Coconut Dressing, 129
   Chicken Salad Bowl with Five-Spice Vinaigrette, 130
   Shrimp-and-Glass Noodle Salad, 148
rice paper wrappers
   Veggie Summer Rolls with Hoisin Peanut Sauce, 72
ricotta cheese
   Lemon-Ricotta Lima Bean Dip, 19
   Simple Beet-and-Arugula Salad with Whipped Ricotta And Honey Vinaigrette, 109
roast beef
   Bahn Mi Sandwiches, 65
   Beefsteak Salad with Blue Cheese-Balsamic Vinaigrette, 137
   Roast Beef Salad with Heirloom Tomatoes and Thai Dressing, 138
   Steak, Corn, and Tomato Salad with Smoky Cumin Vinaigrette, 136
   Watercress-and-Roast Beef Salad with Chimichurri Vinaigrette, 139
Roast Beef Salad with Heirloom Tomatoes and Thai Dressing, 138
Roasted Red Pepper Hummus, 17
   Greek Chicken-and-Zucchini Wrap, 69
Roquefort
   Beet, Orange, and Blue Cheese Salad with Tarragon Vinaigrette, 108
rosemary
   Turkey with Rosemary-Orange Marmalade Sauce, 64
rum
   Bushwacker Shake, 47
   Tiramisu, 158

S

Salad Bowl with Curried Miso Dressing, 135
salads and sides.
   Beet, Orange, and Blue Cheese Salad with Tarragon Vinaigrette, 108
   Bibb Salad with Raspberries, Mango, Hazelnuts, Goat Cheese, and Raspberry Vinaigrette, 107
   Cantaloupe-and-Blueberry Salad with Honey, Lime, and Mint, 92
   Carrot, Mango, and Jicama Slaw, 110
   Cauliflower Chickpea Salad Bowl with Curry-Tahini Dressing, 96
   Celery Salad with Dates, Walnuts, and Parmesan, 94
   Chopped Salad with Avocado-Ranch Dressing, 104
   Couscous-Tabbouleh Salad, 98
   Creamy Cucumber-and-Sweet Onion Salad, 93
   Dilled Egg Salad, 60
   Ham Salad, 63
   Hearts of Palm, Grapefruit, and Avocado Salad, 97
   Heirloom Tomato Panzanella with Brie and Basil, 100–101
   Kale Salad with Orange-Sesame Dressing, 106
   Marinated Celery-and-Chickpea Salad with Lemon-Shallot Vinaigrette, 95
   Marinated Heirloom Tomatoes with Burrata, 89
   Mediterranean White Bean Salad, 99
   Moroccan Kale-and-Grain Salad with Cumin-Coriander Vinaigrette, 102
   No-Cook Chicken Salad Wraps, 70
   Open-faced Avocado-Egg Salad Sandwich, 54
   Ramen Noodle Slaw, 112–113
   Simple Beet-and-Arugula Salad with Whipped Ricotta and Honey Vinaigrette, 109

Simple Side Salad with Blended Ginger Dressing, 105
Strawberry Spinach Salad with Toasted Pecans and Honey-Poppy Seed Dressing, 103
Tex-Mex Coleslaw with Creamy Lime-Chipotle Dressing, 111
Tomato-and-Avocado Salad, 90
Tomato Salad with Herbed Buttermilk Dressing, 88
Wedge Salad with Buttermilk-Blue Cheese Dressing, 91

salami
   Antipasto Salad With Marinated Artichokes, Beans, Slivered Meats, And Creamy Hummus Dressing, 141

salmon
   Quinoa-and-Smoked Salmon Kale Bowl with Lemon-Tahini Dressing, 145
   Smoked Salmon-and-Beet Salad with Gribiche Dressing, 146
   Smoked Salmon Breakfast Wrap, 55
   Smoked Salmon Bruschetta with Arugula Pesto, 26
   Smoked Sockeye Caesar Salad with Lemony Dressing, 144
   Smoky Salmon Dip, 21

sandwiches and wraps
   Bahn Mi Sandwiches, 65
   Chicken, Prosciutto, and Goat Cheese Sandwiches, 67
   Chicken-and-Black Bean Tostadas, 74
   Dilled Egg Salad, 60
   Elevated Cream Cheese-and-Olive Sandwiches, 62
   Greek Chicken-and-Zucchini Wrap, 69
   Ham Salad, 63
   Lemony Lobster Rolls, 66
   Mediterranean Hummus Wrap with Vinaigrette, 68
   No-Cook Chicken Salad Wraps, 70
   Open-faced Avocado-Egg Salad Sandwich, 54
   Pimiento Cheese, 61
   Smoked Salmon Breakfast Wrap, 55
   Spicy Lentil Lettuce Wraps, 73
   Turkey with Rosemary-Orange Marmalade Sauce, 64
   Veggie Summer Rolls with Hoisin Peanut Sauce, 72

sauces and dressings
   Arugula Pesto, 26
   Avocado-Ranch Dressing, 104
   Balsamic Glaze, 22
   Basic Red Wine Vinaigrette, 68
   Blended Ginger Dressing, 105
   Blue Cheese-Balsamic Vinaigrette, 137
   Buttermilk-Blue Cheese Dressing, 91
   Caper-Shallot Vinaigrette, 142
   Chimichurri Vinaigrette, 139
   Chipotle Dressing, 123
   Chipotle Ranch Dressing, 122
   Cilantro-Lime Vinaigrette, 128
   Creamy Chipotle Dressing, 131
   Creamy Green Goddess Dressing, 127
   Creamy Hummus Dressing, 141
   Creamy Lime-Chipotle Dressing, 111
   Cumin-Coriander Vinaigrette, 102
   Curried Miso Dressing, 135
   Curry-Tahini Dressing, 96
   Date Vinaigrette, 143
   Dijon Vinaigrette, 120–121
   Five-Spice Vinaigrette, 130
   Gribiche Dressing, 146
   Herbed Buttermilk Dressing, 88
   Hoisin-Peanut Dipping Sauce, 72
   Honey-Mustard Dressing, 124
   Honey-Orange Dressing, 126
   Honey-Poppy Seed Dressing, 103
   Honey Vinaigrette, 109
   Lemon-Shallot Vinaigrette, 95
   Lemon-Tahini Dressing, 145
   Lemony Dressing, 144
   Mojo Vinaigrette, 140
   Orange-Sesame Dressing, 106
   Peanut-Coconut Dressing, 129
   Quick Cocktail Sauce, 29
   Raspberry Vinaigrette, 107
   Sesame-Soy Vinaigrette, 125
   Smoky Cumin Vinaigrette, 136
   Spicy Rémoulade, 29
   Tarragon Vinaigrette, 108
   Thai Dressing, 138
   Tzatziki Dressing, 132–133

serrano chili
   Thai Dressing, 138

Sesame-Soy Vinaigrette
   Chicken-and-Napa Cabbage Salad with Sesame-Soy Vinaigrette, 125

shallots
   Caper-Shallot Vinaigrette, 142
   Lemon-Shallot Vinaigrette, 95

shrimp
   Chilled Shrimp with Two Sauces, 29
   Cóctel de Camarones, 28
   Shrimp-and-Glass Noodle Salad, 148
   Shrimp-and-Hoppin' John Salad, 149
   Southern Pickled Shrimp, 36–37
   Shrimp-and-Glass Noodle Salad, 148
   Shrimp-and-Hoppin' John Salad, 149

Simple Beet-and-Arugula Salad with Whipped Ricotta and Honey Vinaigrette, 109
Simple Side Salad with Blended Ginger Dressing, 105

skirt steak
   Watercress-and-Roast Beef Salad With Chimichurri Vinaigrette, 139

Smoked Salmon-and-Beet Salad with Gribiche Dressing, 146
Smoked Salmon Breakfast Wrap, 55
Smoked Salmon Bruschetta with Arugula Pesto, 26
Smoked Sockeye Caesar Salad with Lemony Dressing, 144
Smoked Trout Dip, 35
Smoky Cheddar-Pecan Cheese Ball, 27
Smoky Chipotle-Bacon Deviled Eggs, 33

Smoky Cumin Vinaigrette
   Steak, Corn, and Tomato Salad with Smoky Cumin Vinaigrette, 136

Smoky Salmon Dip, 21

snow peas
   Chicken-and-Napa Cabbage Salad with Sesame-Soy Vinaigrette, 125

soups
   All-the-Red-Things Chilled Soup, 82
   Chilled Avocado Soup, 80
   Chilled Cucumber Soup, 79
   Chilled Zucchini-and-Basil Soup, 84
   Golden Tomato-and-Peach Gazpacho, 81
   Spicy Garden Veggie Soup, 78
   White Gazpacho with Cucumber, 85

Southern Chicken, Tomato, and Black-eyed Pea Salad, 119
Southern Pickled Shrimp, 36–37

soy sauce
   Sesame-Soy Vinaigrette, 125

Spicy Chicken-and-Mango Salad Bowl with Cilantro-Lime Vinaigrette, 128
Spicy Garden Veggie Soup, 78
Spicy Lentil Lettuce Wraps, 73

Spicy Rémoulade
   Chilled Shrimp with Two Sauces, 29

spinach
   Strawberry-Spinach Salad with Toasted Pecans And Honey-Poppy Seed Dressing, 103

Steak, Corn, and Tomato Salad with Smoky Cumin Vinaigrette, 136

strawberries
   All-the-Red-Things Chilled Soup, 82
   Berry-Cheesecake Cups, 162
   Gingersnap-and-Berries Tart, 164

Strawberry-Brownie Trifle Cups, 159
Strawberry-Spinach Salad with Toasted Pecans and Honey-Poppy Seed Dressing, 103
Strawberry-Brownie Trifle Cups, 159
Strawberry-Spinach Salad with Toasted Pecans and Honey-Poppy Seed Dressing, 103
Sun-dried Tomato-and-Pesto Torta, 30
Super Quick-and-Easy Peach Sherbet, 155

T

tahini
  Curry-Tahini Dressing, 96
  Lemon-Tahini Dressing, 145
  Roasted Red Pepper Hummus, 17
tarragon
  Chilled Cucumber Soup, 79
  Lemony Herbed Chicken Salad, 116
  Tarragon Vinaigrette, 108
Tarragon Vinaigrette
  Beet, Orange, and Blue Cheese Salad with Tarragon Vinaigrette, 108
Tex-Mex Coleslaw with Creamy Lime-Chipotle Dressing, 111
Thai basil
  No-Cook Chicken Salad Wraps, 70
  Roast Beef Salad with Heirloom Tomatoes and Thai Dressing, 138
Thai Dressing
  Roast Beef Salad with Heirloom Tomatoes and Thai Dressing, 138
Tiki Blush, 44
Tiramisu, 158
tofu
  Veggie Summer Rolls with Hoisin Peanut Sauce, 72
Tomato, White Bean, and Tuna Salad, 99
Tomato-and-Avocado Salad, 90
tomatoes
  All-the-Red-Things Chilled Soup, 82
  Golden Tomato-and-Peach Gazpacho, 81
  Heirloom Tomato Panzanella with Brie and Basil, 100–101
  Marinated Heirloom Tomatoes with Burrata, 89
  Quick, Fresh Heirloom Salsa, 14
  Roast Beef Salad with Heirloom Tomatoes and Thai Dressing, 138
  Southern Chicken, Tomato, and Black-eyed Pea Salad, 119
  Spicy Garden Veggie Soup, 78
  Steak, Corn, and Tomato Salad with Smoky Cumin Vinaigrette, 136
Tomato, White Bean, and Tuna Salad, 99
Tomato-and-Avocado Salad, 90
Tomato Salad with Herbed Buttermilk Dressing, 88
Tomato Salad with Herbed Buttermilk Dressing, 88
tortillas
  Greek Chicken-and-Zucchini Wrap, 69
  Mediterranean Hummus Wrap with Vinaigrette, 68
  Mexican Chicken Cobb Salad with Chipotle Ranch Dressing, 122
  Smoked Salmon Breakfast Wrap, 55
  Steak, Corn, and Tomato Salad with Smoky Cumin Vinaigrette, 136
Tropical Sangría, 42
trout
  Fall Greens with Smoked Trout, Pear, Cranberry, and Date Vinaigrette, 143
  Smoked Trout Dip, 35
tuna
  Tomato, White Bean, and Tuna Salad, 99
  Tuna Niçoise Salad with Caper-Shallot Vinaigrette, 142
Tuna Niçoise Salad With Caper-Shallot Vinaigrette, 142
Turkey with Rosemary-Orange Marmalade Sauce, 64
Tzatziki Dressing
  Greek Chicken Rice Bowl with Tzatziki Dressing, 132–133

V

vanilla almond milk
  Brown Sugar-Cinnamon Overnight Oatmeal, 53
  Creamy Kale-and-Cashew Smoothie, 52
vanilla ice cream
  Bushwacker Shake, 47
vanilla pudding mix
  No-Bake Banana Cream Pie with Chocolate Layer, 166
  Strawberry-Brownie Trifle Cups, 159
vegetable juice
  Cóctel de Camarones, 28
  Spicy Garden Veggie Soup, 78
vegetables, 7, 9, 10. See also specific types
Veggie Summer Rolls with Hoisin Peanut Sauce, 72
vodka
  Tropical Sangría, 42

W

walnuts
  Celery Salad with Dates, Walnuts, and Parmesan, 94
  Chicken Waldorf Salad, 118
washing produce, 10
watercress
  Hearty Cuban Salad with Mojo Vinaigrette, 140
  Watercress-and-Roast Beef Salad with Chimichurri Vinaigrette, 139
Watercress-and-Roast Beef Salad With Chimichurri Vinaigrette, 139
watermelon
  All-the-Red-Things Chilled Soup, 82
  Watermelon Agua Fresca, 41
  Watermelon-Feta-Cucumber Bites with Balsamic Glaze, 22
Watermelon Agua Fresca, 41
Watermelon-Feta-Cucumber Bites with Balsamic Glaze, 22
Wedge Salad with Buttermilk-Blue Cheese Dressing, 91
West Indies Crab Salad, 34
whipping cream. See heavy cream
Whiskey Amaretto Slushie, 49
white beans
  Mediterranean White Bean Salad, 99
  Tomato, White Bean, and Tuna Salad, 99
White Gazpacho With Cucumber, 85
White Linen Cocktail, 43
white miso paste
  Curried Miso Dressing, 135
white rice
  Shrimp-and-Hoppin' John Salad, 149
white wine
  Tropical Sangría, 42

Y

yellow rice
  Chicken Burrito Bowl with Creamy Chipotle Dressing, 131
yellow squash
  Mediterranean White Bean Salad, 99

Z

Za'Atar Chicken, Bulgur, and Lentil Salad Bowl, 134
zucchini
  Chilled Zucchini-and-Basil Soup, 84
  Greek Chicken-and-Zucchini Wrap, 69
  Spicy Garden Veggie Soup, 78

Cover design by Hilary Harkness
Book design by Hilary Harkness
Edited by Emily Beaumont

Cover images: All photos copyright by **Julia Rutland** unless otherwise noted.

All photos by **Julia Rutland** unless otherwise noted.

Images used under license from Shutterstock.com:
Ailisa: 91 (carrots); **akepong srichaichana:** 78 (zucchini); **AlenKadr:** 5 (immersion blender, glass container, canning jars); **Alesia.Bierliezova:** 175 (salad greens); **Alina Kholopova:** viii; **Amalgamka:** 168 (chocolate curls); **Anna Norcross:** vii; **Anton Starikov:** 5 (cutting board), 148; **Arantxa Forcada Garcia:** 179 (lemons); **arpho visual:** 14 (tomatoes); **ArtKio:** grainy background on pages 9, 174–175, 176–177, and 178–179; **AtlasStudio:** 111 (corn); **Avocado_studio:** 23; **Azan1515:** 158 (ladyfingers); **baibaz:** i, 56 (coconut); **bergamont:** 166 (banana), 171 (chocolate); **by Artists:** 172 (coffee); **CHZU:** 176 (cutting boards/bowls); **Danny Smythe:** 168 (cream cheese); **DENYSOFF:** 18 (pineapple); **Diana Taliun:** 89 (tomatoes); **domnitsky:** 120 (red onion); **Emily C. McCormick:** 2; **Esin Deniz:** 30 (pine nuts); **FASTRO:** 5 (blender); **Food Impressions:** 28 (shrimp); **Freebird7977:** ii–iii (background image); **Galayko Sergey:** 74 (black beans); **George3973:** 138 (cashews); **gresei:** 20 (walnuts), 70 (butter lettuce); **GSDesign:** 85 (shallots), 90 (avocado), 132 (dill, 144 (salmon); **Gv Image-1:** 162 (blueberries); **HAKINMHAN:** v; **Holiday.Photo.Top:** 106 (raspberries); **Hong Vo:** 61 (cheddar cheese), 150 (green onion); **hsagencia:** 100 (olives); **Jack_the_sparow:** 5 (peeler); **jensen77:** 5 (mandolin); **JIANG HONGYAN:** 125 (snow peas); **Joe Gough:** 26 (salmon); **Kaiskynet Studio:** 43 (lemon slices); **Katerina Maksymenko:** 23 (basil); **Louella938:** 24 (blue cheese); **mahirart:** 172 (pecans); **Maks Peoplenko:** 128 (mango); **MarcoFood:** 36 (garlic), 82 (strawberries), 167 (peanuts); **marekuliasz:** 75 (grape tomatoes), 177 (measuring spoons); **matkub2499:** 125 (red cabbage); **Maxwell Photography:** 172 (dates); **Meilan Photography:** 100 (brie); **Melanie Hobson:** 134 (lentils); **MERCURY studio:** 82 (beet); **Nataly Studio:** 120 (garlic); **Nataly Zavyalova:** 68 (tomatoes); **Nature522:** 5 (bowls); **New Africa:** 5 (vacuum sealer), 10, 19 (lemon), 29 (lemon), 56 (almond butter), 62 (dill), 104 (bacon), 112 (cranberries), 132 (garlic), 140 (arugula); **Phongphan:** 125 (napa cabbage); **Photoongraphy:** 28 (avocado), 70 (red onion), 85 (grapes); **Photour.1904:** 56 (quick oats); **Pinkyone:** barnboards on pages 13, 39, 51, 59, 77, 87, 115, 153, 174–175, 176–177, 178–179; **Pixel-Shot:** 78 (yellow bell pepper); **pukao:** 36 (parsley), 107 (kale); **Quang Ho:** 41 (watermelon); **Satria_Photo:** 99 (cannellini beans); **showcake:** 56 (chocolate chips); **siriratsavett:** 41 (lime); **Snowbelle:** 16 (whole cranberries); **Steven Urquhart:** 5 (juicer); **Subject Photo:** 150 (celery); **Tanya_mtv:** 70 (jalepeno); **Tarasyuk Igor:** 111 (cabbage); **Target Shot:** 5 (salad spinner); **TatianaMishina:** 88 (thyme); **The Athenian:** 5 (microplane); **Tiger Images:** 62 (olives); **Tim UR:** 61 (onion); **Valentyn Volkov:** 17 (red bell pepper); **Vas_Kondr:** 159 (strawberries); **vblinov:** 5 (food processor); **Vicushka:** 97 (grapefruit); **Washdog:** 192 (frame background); **XMai Images:** 43 (cucumber); **Yana Bo:** 17 (chickpeas); **YARUNIV Studio:** 7; **Yasonya:** 190 (flowers); **years44:** 127 (tomatoes)

10 9 8 7 6 5 4 3 2 1

Some Assembly Required
Copyright © 2026 by Julia Rutland
Published by Adventure Publications
An imprint of AdventureKEEN
310 Garfield Street South
Cambridge, Minnesota 55008
(800) 678-7006
www.adventurepublications.net
All rights reserved
Printed in China
LCCN 2025048561 (print); 2025048562 (ebook)
ISBN 978-1-64755-540-5 (pbk.); ISBN 978-1-64755-541-2 (ebook)

The Story of AdventureKEEN

We are an independent nature and outdoor activity publisher. Our founding dates back more than 40 years, guided then and now by our love of being in the woods and on the water, by our passion for reading and books, and by the sense of wonder and discovery made possible by spending time recreating outdoors in beautiful places.

It is our mission to share that wonder and fun with our readers, especially with those who haven't yet experienced all the physical and mental health benefits that nature and outdoor activity can bring.

In addition, we strive to teach about responsible recreation so that the natural resources and habitats we cherish and rely upon will be available for future generations.

We are a small team deeply rooted in the places where we live and work. We have been shaped by our communities of origin—primarily Birmingham, Alabama; Cincinnati, Ohio; and the northern suburbs of Minneapolis, Minnesota. Drawing on the decades of experience of our staff and our awareness of the industry, the marketplace, and the world at large, we have shaped a unique vision and mission for a company that serves our readers and authors.

We hope to meet you out on the trail someday.

#bewellbeoutdoors

ABOUT THE AUTHOR

Julia Rutland is a writer and cookbook author with more than 25 years of experience in food, publishing, travel, and marketing. She has written over a dozen cookbooks, including *The Campfire Foodie Cookbook, On a Stick, Blueberries, Squash, Apples, Honey, Tomatoes, Eggs, Mushrooms, Foil Pack Dinners, 101 Lasagnas, The Christmas Movie Cookbook, Homestyle Kitchen,* and *Cast-Iron Cooking*. Julia is a member of Les Dames d'Escoffier, an international organization of women leaders in food, beverage, and hospitality. She also volunteers with the Virginia Cooperative Extension Master Gardener program, where she serves on the board in Loudoun County. Julia lives in the wine-country town of Hillsboro, Virginia, just outside of Washington, D.C.

Collect the series!